What We Should Teach Our Children About Money

Joshua Fulenwider

DEDICATION

This book is dedicated to my daughter, Ashla. I hope that through this book I can give her an advantage when it comes to thinking about money. She was my inspiration and the first person to read it.

CONTENTS

ACKNOWLEDGMENTS

This book would not have been possible without my daughter, Ashla, who served as inspiration and was the first editor. Getting this book ready to publish is all thanks to my wife, Rebecca, who understands formatting documents, grammar, and punctuation way better than I do and was supportive when I announced randomly that I was going to quit my job and figure the rest out later.

INTRODUCTION

Have you ever hit rock bottom? Where you've felt so miserable and worthless? A failure and a waste of space? Do you know there is a better life out there for you, but you just don't know how to get it? While I can't teach you how to lead a perfect life, I can show you the tools to help you create one with more financial understanding, stability, and wealth. The chapters in this book will provide you with the tools to make better financial decisions, save money, and experience less financial stress. How can I promise all this? Because I've lived it.

In 2004, I was unemployed and struggling with depression. After failing miserably at the career, I had pursued after high school, I felt like I was a burden on my wife. If the insurance policy had paid out in the event of suicide, I would have ended my life. I felt my wife deserved a fresh start after following me into the abyss.

We fought constantly, and money issues were a big part of it. It was so bad that I would have left, but I didn't have anywhere to go. I had lost contact with my friends over the last year, my parents were in the middle of a divorce, and the rest of my extended family was spread out across the country. My wife and I had one car that we shared, and since she was working, she was the one using it. If I had left, I wouldn't even have a car to sleep in.

People told us that it was common for newlyweds to fight. So, we stuck together, and we fought… and fought… and fought. We fought about stupid stuff, but really it was about my struggling with my self-worth. It was at that time when I decided to never feel stuck again and never feel like a failure.

While I still struggle with seeing that period as anything but a massive collapse, life has taught me to look at things as positive as one can. The truth is it forced me to reevaluate my life and the decisions I had made. I had to realize that my plans for my future were not shattered but altered. It changed my personality as I went from being an extrovert to being rather introverted, which gave me more insight into myself and the time to work on myself. Then, I didn't want to do anything. But now, I know I have the power within myself to achieve what I set my mind to.

Eventually, I got through it. At the time, I didn't know much about anything, but I decided that I would pursue success however it came to me. To me, success has always been measured in dollars. It's an easy unit of measurement. But I didn't know very much about money other than I should save for a rainy day and spend less than what I make.

I set out to learn everything about the way money works and how to be successful with it. I've always loved games, and creating money and wealth became a game. I just had to learn the rules. I posed a lot of questions to many different people. Through this, I learned from my parents more than what they had told me in my younger years. My wife shared some things that she had learned from her parents. And I also began pursuing knowledge elsewhere.

Over the past sixteen years, I made it my mission to learn as much as possible about this game that uses money to keep score. I got a degree in business because it related to making money. I worked for a payday lender, a tax preparation company, and eventually got into banking. All these experiences have helped me learn the rules of the game. And then, I began to see how this knowledge could be used for my advantage. During this time, we bought a home and eventually began investing in rental properties and other real estate. I left a good career to pursue passions fueled by the wealth we had created and started a couple of businesses. As I did this, I kept reading books and attending webinars, workshops, meetings, and various training sessions.

What I have learned through my experiences and interactions is that many people don't understand most of the basic things about money. They don't understand what the numbers on their paycheck stand for, don't know how to set up a retirement savings account, and don't have enough knowledge about taxes. A lot is simple, but a lot is overlooked.

And so I decided to write this book for my daughter. I believe she needs to know all she can about money and business in order to get ahead in life just like I have. If you've picked up this book, you're probably looking for ways to give you and your family every possible advantage in life. That's the first step—taking action to look for ways to change. Throughout everything I have experienced, I truly have grown to understand how mindset really frames your path and can guide you. In high school, my mindset was to pursue a path of stability and let others make decisions for me. Therefore, a career in the Navy seemed appealing. If I hadn't failed at it, I would not have gotten to where I am now. I encourage you to look at your journey the same way. There may be shameful things in your past, but what truly matters is the steps you take in making a better life for yourself.

Now my mindset is one of growth, opportunities, and understanding that life is full of ambiguity. There are no wrong answers in life; however, some answers are better than others. I hope I can share some of this with you. I believe that becoming aware of different tools to manage money can guide you to becoming financially stable and wealthy. This book is a jumping-off point and will help start you on your own journey to riches.

How You Can Use This Book

I applaud you if you've picked up this book for yourself. It's packed with information to help people of all ages. There are additional ways to further your understanding of certain topics and be able to hear other perspectives. I encourage you to do the following:

1. Discuss the topics you're working on with like-minded people. If you want to become rich, surround yourself with others who have the same desire and are putting in the effort to make a change.
2. See whether you can join a book club and read through a book and have discussions together.
3. In a relationship? What better time than now to start these discussions with your potential life partner!

If you chose this book to teach your kids about money, there are three ways to go about it:

1. Give it to your child to read in hopes that they read it and learn from it. This is the least effective.
2. Read it yourself and then discuss it with your child and try to teach them what's in the book. This is vastly more effective. You will learn

the principles yourself so much better by trying to teach it to someone else. This is also a great way to spend time with your kids and can even be a bridge to conversation if you're struggling to connect on things.

3.   Both you and your child read it and discuss it. This is the most effective. I recommend trying to read one chapter a week and then coming together over a meal to discuss what you've learned.

No matter how you read it, I hope you find value in what I have written and find a way to share it with others.

I wrote this book in a specific order because I believe that each chapter builds a foundation for the following chapter. However, I won't take offense if you skip around or don't read certain sections. I've tried to touch on everything that I think is most critical to achieving financial success, but this book is not comprehensive on any single subject. I must admit that there are some areas in here that I'm not an expert on. However, I think everyone should know the basic structures of different types of accounts, the tax implications, and what type of instruments are available. It is my sincere hope that you and your child learn enough from this book so that you can start on the path to financial success.

At the beginning of every chapter are excerpts of conversations I have had with my daughter, Ashla, about money. I did my best to write them down as I remember them. They take place anywhere from her being about four years old up to the age of fourteen (the time of this writing). Ashla has a great sense of humor, and there is a lot of joking around in our house. When you read our conversations, keep that in mind to get the correct tone.

You'll notice a lot of footnotes. A few of them are references, but the majority of them are not. Some of them seek to explain a word or concept in more detail when it didn't fit in with the structure of what I was saying. Other footnotes include some additional thoughts I had on the subject. I encourage you to at least glance at the footnotes as you come across them to help deepen your understanding.

Throughout this book, I share my life stories that, I believe, are relevant to the point being made and help frame my mindset in approaching money. Even though the chapters build on each other sequentially, the stories in them don't follow any sort of order.

A quick disclaimer: Any examples of forms in this book are for educational purposes only, and many of them are updated every year (especially those in chapter 8 on taxes). If you want a more recent copy of the forms, a quick internet search should help you find the current versions. You should also seek competent legal, tax, or financial advice before making investment decisions.

1: WINNERS WIN

"What do winners do, Ashla?" I asked my daughter.
"They win!" she replied.

This idea is at the start of the book, because I think it is the most important. Winners win. It seems simple enough, but it captures and summarizes an idea that people around me have tried to put into words for years. In order to succeed, you should first have the right mindset in approaching the rest of your life.

Chances are you've heard the following advice throughout your life: get good grades, graduate from high school, participate in extracurricular activities and do well in them, join clubs and advance as high as you can, go to college, finish college (preferably in four years), volunteer, get a job, advance in your job, and more.

"Why should I do all these things?" you may be asking yourself. I get it. When I was coming out of high school, all I wanted to do was to go into the Navy and travel the world. The military doesn't need superstars. They don't care that I was in theatre club in high school or that I almost made it to Eagle Scout. If they don't care, why should I?

Because winners win. This is a simplified statement that can propel you to achieve so much more in your life than you were planning on. It took me years to fully understand the concept, but I didn't have words for it. It wasn't until I was in my thirties that I heard this phrase and instantly knew that it summed up a ton of the self-help information I read and studied after I had left the Navy.

I was planning to work for twenty years in the Navy and then retire, but my plans ended abruptly after only three months in Naval Training due to an unforeseen medical concern. My plans changed. Life changes and we never know when, where, or how. I didn't plan on my time in the Navy being as short as it was. I hadn't been purposefully trying to build my resume or succeed at life prior to the Navy. The clubs, sports, and activities I had done were for fun but never meant to help me develop skills. Fortunately, they did teach me things and helped me develop skills.

After having been on countless interviews and now having interviewed countless people as an employer, I have come to believe that the actual content of a person's resume isn't as important as the trend that it illustrates. As the employer, I like to see people who are motived and can succeed at whatever they set their mind to.

Someone that changes jobs every six months but has just been doing the same thing for the past ten years isn't a winner. But they aren't necessarily a loser either.

Someone that changes jobs every six months in the same profession but has been going to school, supporting a family, paying off debt, working on a side hustle is someone that has proven that they can be successful.

After the Navy, I went back to college because my parents thought I needed a college education to get a good job—even if the degree was in underwater basket weaving. They said my having the degree would show employers that I was smart and could finish things, that employers were looking for college graduates, and that I would need it to get ahead. I'm still not sure how deciding on a degree in underwater basket weaving could be seen as a smart move, but off to college I went.

To this day, not a single employer has ever asked me about my college education.

My parents were right, but for the wrong reasons. The best reason for going to college (besides the parties and dating scene) was that it demonstrated to others, but more importantly to myself, that I could succeed at something I set my mind to. What greater statement is there than to say, "I spent years of late nights and hard work, sacrificing time with friends or earning money, to accomplish this"!

The same can be said for attaining the rank of Eagle Scout, a black belt in karate, or mastering a musical instrument. Before they are achieved, all these things take years of concentrated effort, a lot of practice, and countless small failures.

Change in Mindset

So why should you show up, participate, and strive to excel in all the different areas of life? What does it show? How will it help you?

- GET GOOD GRADES: It demonstrates that you are either smart or hard working. You don't have to be a straight A student. I wasn't. We all have different abilities and strengths, but doing well means putting in the effort, staying late for tutoring, and completing test corrections or extra credit if offered.

- GRADUATE FROM HIGH SCHOOL: This is a life accomplishment that you should be proud of. This shows you can complete a twelve-year (give or take) commitment to something. It can get hard towards the end, but I promise the benefits outweigh the quick-fix solution of dropping out.

- PARTICIPATE IN EXTRACURRICULAR ACTIVITIES: These activities build new skills, especially in team settings, and demonstrate your commitment. Most schools offer a variety of activities, including sports, band, drama, stage crew, etc. Communities also offer activities, including dance, karate, archery, etc., and can be found at community centers, libraries, or local businesses.

- JOIN CLUBS: Clubs are a bit more social in their interaction than extracurricular activities, but many clubs have a mission they are focused on achieving, while athletic or musical skills are not needed. Joining clubs allows you to meet new people and learn new things. These can be inside of school or as part of your community and can include art, physics club, dance crew, Girl or Boy Scouts, 4H, etc. Many clubs outside of school, such as Lions or Kiwanis, are focused on specific missions of volunteerism.

- ADVANCE IN CLUBS: Beyond just showing up, be present. Advancement can be achieving higher awards or being a part of committees. This demonstrates to the rest of the world your ability to succeed and that you take your commitments seriously.

- VOLUNTEER: Food banks, community events, school events, etc. Get out there, give back, and learn more about your community and how it runs. This shows the rest of the world that you care about more than just yourself and opens you up to a network of new people. You'll also learn skills that you otherwise wouldn't have, which may end up being very helpful later in life.

- GET A JOB: Having any job experience is better than none. You can start small with babysitting or mowing lawns for neighbors, but you gain a great sense of how to treat people and how you want to be treated if you venture into entry level customer service or labor environments while still in high school. Being a productive member of society is something you will be judged on your whole life but should also be something you strive to achieve.

- GO TO COLLEGE: College isn't for everyone, so investigate ways you can further your education that works for you. Trade schools and Unions are great ways for hands-on learners to gain extra experience too. Advancing your education will expose you to a world of new ideas and people. It will open up possibilities to travel as part of your education and post-education experience.

- FINISH COLLEGE: Everyone's college experience can be different, whether it's a two-year community college, a four-year university, or longer to obtain a masters. The important part is to commit to finishing a degree. It's never too late to return to college, but make sure the first time you go to commit to finishing a benchmark. To the rest of the world, this demonstrates your ability to follow through on big projects. It demonstrates your ability to learn and work hard. It is also something you can be proud of accomplishing.

- ADVANCE IN YOUR JOB: Don't be happy at the bottom. Starting at minimum wage gets you in the door, but I bet you'd prefer to earn much more money. Advancement typically brings money. Strive to become an opening or closing crew member, a shift lead, a trainer, a manager, etc. If management isn't an option or not your thing, you can still strive to do your job with the best attitude and go above and beyond to do it better than anyone else. Advancing in your job makes you more desirable to other employers that will see you as a leader, driven, or very capable.

- ETC: What are you passionate about and involved in or want to be right now? How can you advance within this? What else could you be proud of and tell others about?

At the end of the day, you should push to do well in all that you do, because people know that Winners Win!

Why I Want My Daughter to Know This

At this point, my daughter rolls her eyes whenever I say ,"Winners Win!" After all, she has heard it so many times. She understands that taking any situation, especially a less desirable one, and refocusing your mindset on how it will help you achieve your goals, move you forward, or benefit you is the basis of the statement.

We have always had a healthy competition in our house even before coming across this phrase. The phrase just helped us explain our constant pushing for success across all the activities we do.

I want my daughter to know this so she finds the value in understanding that success in little things leads to success in big things. On my tough days, I always sense a little glimmer of hope that my words are getting through when I am struggling to change my mindset and she looks at me with a straight face and says, "Winners win, Dad."

2: WORK PRINCIPLES

"I want to quit karate," Ashla told me one day.

"Why?" I asked, feeling that this was coming out of the blue.

"I want to do other things like dance and gymnastics, and karate takes too much time." Karate was monopolizing three-four nights a week.

"You have been doing it three and a half years," I stated. "You are only six months away from getting your junior black belt."

"I don't really care about that anymore. I really want to do gymnastics."

"Ashla, there are very few times in your life when I am going to push you to do something. This is going to be one of those times. You are over 85 percent of the way to finishing a major accomplishment that you can be proud of for the rest of your life. No one will be able to take it away from you..."

"I don't care," she stated. "I don't want to do it anymore."

I tried not to let our tempers rise and proposed a solution. "What if we find a way to add gymnastics to your schedule but cutting back just a bit on karate? Once you get to your black belt, you can give it a rest."

"But why?"

"There will be times in your life when you'll want to prove to other people that you can do things. If you haven't proven to yourself that you can finish hard things, you won't stand a chance of proving them to anyone else. By finishing a major achievement, like your black belt, you will know the rest of your life that you have the ability to start a project that may take years and see it finished."

She stuck out her tongue but then said, "Okay."

Someone smarter than me once came up with a list of work principles[1] that require zero skills. This chapter contains parts of that list along with some of

---

[1] A principle is a rule or truth that people's beliefs are based on. For example, some principles help people determine right from wrong.

my own. These are things anyone can do. You don't need to have a college degree or even a high school education. You may not have the training or experience necessary. You might have a criminal offense on your record. You could have everything in the world going against you. But if you do these things, you vastly increase the probability that your employer will be happy with you.

Timeliness

Let's start off by saying that you should aim to be always on time.

Nothing peeves an employer and coworkers more than a tardy person. Being late once is excusable. Twice is irritating. Anything more than that just illustrates your inability to manage your time. Worse, others think you place greater value on your time than they place on theirs. Being late is selfish.

There are special times when you should ensure you are never late. For instance, if you just started a new job you should never be late for the first three months. Most of the time, you are under probation during this time frame, and a habit of tardiness will likely result in your being terminated.

It is even more important to be on time during peak seasons for your work. If you work in retail, an example of this would be during the holidays. Your employer will definitely notice when people are late during times of high volume. A tardy person will not go unnoticed when the boss is super busy.

While you may just be an employee, it is good to understand your boss's perspective. Employers are constantly struggling to balance schedules, especially if it is hourly work. They need the right number of staff working to deal with a variety of expected customer surges through the day or week. For restaurants, these revolve around meals. A labor job may start each morning with a group meeting to assign tasks and divvy up the work for the day. Retail jobs may experience customer surges in the evening or after community events. For banks, surges may be around lunchtime and at the end of the day, on Fridays, and at the beginning/end of the month. A person that is consistently tardy makes it difficult to plan for adequate staffing.

Your being tardy may push other employees into overtime, which can add stress to the employer. It also makes your coworkers late for their own personal commitments—doctor appointments, their kid's soccer games, or just getting home for dinner.

A tardy person adds stress to those around them. There may be times when being late is truly unavoidable, such as being in an accident. However, you should plan your time well enough to take minor delays into account. If you notice that you keep experiencing traffic delays, you should leave your house earlier. If your significant other sometimes takes a longer shower, maybe you should get up a couple of minutes earlier to compensate for it. Employers would rather have someone that always shows up a few minutes early than someone who comes in late once a week.

Good Effort

Walk into any place of employment and ask someone who the hardest worker is, and they can tell you. If you ask them who the laziest worker is, they can tell you that, too.

Putting in effort is hard work. It's fun to chat with your coworkers and take a break for a moment. But if there is still work to be done you should be doing it. You can become known as the person who gets things done just because you are working while others are socializing.

You need to focus on being efficient in your work without cutting corners.[2] Cut back on unnecessary things, such as too many coffee breaks. Another thing you could do to help with this would be to rearrange or prep your workspace so you don't spend as much time looking for what you need while you work.

You also need to work quickly. Don't dawdle (meaning move slowly to purposefully waste time). Walk with purpose and get to where you are going. Good servers in restaurants develop this skill naturally. When they are busy, they flit around the restaurant quickly so they can get to more tables and provide better service, thereby increasing their tips. No matter what industry you're in, watch a good server the next time you go out to eat. Then mimic the speed with which they work.

Putting in good effort can lead to opportunities to learn new things and attend special training. After being a lender for about a year, I was asked to attend an advanced banking school by the bank I worked for. The school taught bankers in various roles about advanced concepts involving portfolio management, pricing loans and deposits, credit theory, and more. It was an honor to be asked to attend and meant a lot to me that the bank would pay to

---

[2] *Cutting corners* means you try to rush a job by doing it in the easiest and fastest way but also leave something important out. For a famous example of cutting corners, look up the movie *Deepwater Horizon*.

further my education. The bank viewed the money being spent as an investment in someone (me) that would make the most out of the opportunity, do the required work, and bring new ideas and skills back to the company and applying it to my job.

Body Language

Always portray confidence and openness in your body language at work. Make sure you stand or sit up tall as opposed to being slouched or hunched. Display openness by turning your body to face those whom you are speaking to. Make eye contact (or look at the tip of their nose if eye contact is too intimidating).

Show interest by pointing your toes towards the person or object of your attention. This is also a good indicator if you are talking with someone, and they are wanting to end the conversation. If their toes are pointed away from you, find a way to wind the conversation down and release them (and yourself).

If you are speaking with someone you want to like you, slightly mimic their body language. If they are leaning forward, you lean forward too. If they have their hands on the desk, you should as well. There are times when you don't want to mimic the other person's body language, and this is when theirs is bad. If they have their arms crossed and are closed off to the conversation, you want to be open in return. If this is just a mood, you may be able to draw them out of it. If it is the other person's personality, then do you really need or want them to like you? You don't want to do exactly what they do, but if you mimic them enough, they will unconsciously view you as similar to themselves and because they like themselves, they'll be more likely to like you.

Energy

My wife is the master of energy. She is always upbeat and has energy to spare. This comes naturally to her. For me, I have had to work at it.

I spent some time learning about Neuro-Linguistic Programming (NLP)[3]

---

[3] NLP is the process of utilizing your words and thoughts to determine your reality. By modelling your thoughts and words after other successful people's thoughts and words you should be able to achieve similar results. To learn more, visit https://www.goodtherapy.org/learn-about-therapy/types/neuro-linguistic-

and applying practices to my life. I tell myself internally and sometimes out loud the feelings I want to have. If I want to have energy, I tell myself I have energy. I don't punish myself and stress about not being able to fall asleep or waking up before my alarm. This is just my body's way of telling me, "I am already rested enough, and I don't need as much sleep." In a nutshell, you actively use your mind to tell yourself how to feel.

If that sounds a little hokey, I understand. There are times I struggle with it as well, but I believe in sharing ideas that may work for others. It may work for you. If it doesn't work, try having that extra cup of coffee to help perk you up. You can also try physical activity. Getting out for a short walk is a great reset for when you are feeling drained. Sleep as much or little as you need to around your work day. The point is to do your best not to punish yourself if you can't sleep.

Having energy in all that you do shows your eagerness to do good work. People like to be around those with energy. Furthermore, energy is often contagious, and you can spread an upbeat or downtrodden energy through your workplace. What type of environment would you rather work in?

Attitude

Attitude and energy go together. It's much easier to have a lot of energy if you bring positivity to all you do. Being positive, negative, or neutral is a choice. And it is a choice only you can make.

No one can force you to be in a good or bad mood. Many times, I hear people complain about what their boss or coworker did to them. This causes a bad mood or negative outlook. You can't control other people's actions. You can control your reaction.

People with a negative outlook on life have an external *locus of control.* Locus of control is the proper term for when people believe control exists in their life—either within themselves or by forces outside their control. Many people with negative attitudes who like to complain and always seem to be victims of everything believe heavily that the circumstances of their life are outside of their ability to control.

Conversely, when someone has a positive attitude, they often believe that they can directly affect their surroundings. This means they have an internal locus of control.[4] It is much easier to be positive when you believe that each

programming.

decision you make and the work that you do can make your life better. No one wants to be around a "Debbie Downer." I encourage you to be a champion of positivity.

Passion

Pour everything you have into your job. When I worked in an ice cream store, I made sure it was the best ice cream store I could make it. I learned everything I could about the business in the hopes of being a part of making it run better.

When I became a commercial lender, I wanted to be a great lender. I would read about banking, economics, and about my customer's industries constantly. I read the business section of news sites to stay on top of current events that were affecting my borrowers. Then I would read business books so I could better understand the problems being faced by my customers and provide guidance.

Reading was not enough to fulfill my desire to be great at my job. So, I attended classes and listened to the advice and experiences of those around me. I sought feedback from my customers, peers, and bosses and incorporated that into my work so I could get better. Anything I could do to be better at my job, I did. I learned everything I could to become the best commercial lender that I knew how.

This didn't mean I was always great at what I did. However, because I cared about the outcomes, my mistakes and shortcomings were mostly forgiven and used as an opportunity to grow.

I didn't start off loving either job. Working as a grunt in an ice cream job is mostly thankless and sticky. Being a lender was more responsibility and more stressful. While I worked at all my jobs, I acted as though I loved doing them, and eventually I developed a love for them and a love for the way that I contributed. This also helped me develop a positive attitude and keep my energy level up.

---

[4] I'm not a psychologist. If you want to learn more, visit https://www.psychologytoday.com/us/blog/moments-matter/201708/locus-control.

Coachable

Being open to feedback means that you can listen to other people when they criticize what you are doing. You seek to understand what they are saying and why what you are doing may be incorrect. You can then take it a step further by being coachable. After understanding the criticism, you ask for better ways to do things and then try to incorporate them into what you do.

It is difficult to hear that you are doing something wrong, but this is when you will learn the most. One of my greatest struggles when I was a commercial lender was being tough on people when collecting loans that had gone bad. I was repeatedly criticized by my superior for being unable to squeeze blood from a stone, meaning I could not get customers to do what they really did not want to do. I was forced to learn skills and tactics in being tough with people.

When working at an ice cream store, I was nearly fired because I came across as arrogant to my shift managers. It was humbling to be told this. So, I used it as an opportunity to learn how to be confident and direct instead. I was able to work on myself and develop better interpersonal skills.

In both scenarios, I was told what my shortcomings were. I was also given tools, learned some tools on my own, and I was also given time to work on them.

Being coachable and open to feedback can really pay off. While still a new lender I was asked to attend an advanced banking by a boss that had been mentoring me. He saw that I would make good use of advanced training, because I had taken in all his coaching. I had proven that I could take feedback and make the most of coaching.

That's why, I think, it is so important to be open to feedback. It's okay to ask for help and guidance as well. This displays your willingness to learn and grow in your job.

When someone does give you feedback or advice, take the time to think it through. When measuring the usefulness of feedback, try to judge whether the person is better at their job than you, the information comes from a place of wanting to see you do better, and this feedback or advice is ethical. If it meets all these metrics, then you should try internalizing the information so you can perform better at your job.

By acting on feedback, you should be able to accomplish more in your job.

Do Extra

What is considered "above and beyond" at your job? Is it taking out the trash at the end of the night or rolling extra silverware during slow times at a restaurant?

I once retiled the floor under the sink at the ice cream store. I knew how to do it and got it done for a fraction of the cost that a professional could have gotten it done for. When I was a commercial lender, helping clean up the dirty coffee cups in the sink wasn't beneath me. Once you are done with your work, see what else you can do to make the place better and do it.

This makes everyone else's life easier, and it will not go unnoticed. Chances are, it won't really make your life harder either.

Re-grouting the floor allowed me to flex my home-improvement skills that I hadn't used in a while and made me feel accomplished. Cleaning coffee cups occasionally was a welcome distraction from much more stressful work.

It isn't any harder to do extra, but you will stand out from the rest of the employees when you do. Do it with a positive attitude, and you will feel good too.

Be Prepared

Show up to your day with the proper uniform or attire (including name badge). If your job requires you to have certain tools, make sure you've got them. Complete all your paperwork ahead of time. Be knowledgeable about what you do and the current status of any projects you are working on. If you are in a meeting and called upon to answer questions, be ready to respond.

Being prepared also means ready to work. Show up with the mindset that you are going to get stuff done. You are there to kick butt and take names. If you show up ready to work, you will get more done than those that need to ease into their workday after a cup of coffee or two.

You need to manage yourself outside of work so that you can always perform at your best. Don't show up hungover. Don't show up smelly or dirty (unless that's a job requirement). Don't clock in until you are ready to work (personal items like your coat and keys should be put away, and you should have your name badge on already). When you clock in, you should be ready to immediately get to work. Show up to work sober, clean, and ready to work.

Being prepared often starts the day before you show up for work. Getting a good night's sleep so you aren't tired is important. Being tired will destroy a lot of the good you are trying to do throughout the other principles. Make sure you are well rested.

All these things prepare you to get started. You also need to be prepared for the fact that you won't know everything. Prepare yourself for when and how you will ask questions so that you can do your job. While many people see this as a need only when you are starting a new job, the truth of the matter is you will constantly need to learn because your job will continue to change. Even a simple cashier job is different today from what it was twenty years ago. The way people pay is different, the technology is different, and the items being sold are different. While it is hard to prepare yourself for change, you can be prepared to ask questions so that you can learn new things.

Finish What You Start

As I illustrated at the beginning of this chapter, some projects are hard and take a long time. Finishing such tasks demonstrates your perseverance to others and to yourself. At the end, there is a sense of relief and accomplishment.

When I was a commercial lender, the amount of time I spent working on a single project kept growing. Making a complex loan to a customer could take as long as a year. Working out of a bad loan or collecting could require several years. These weren't the only types of projects I did, but they lasted a long time. They weren't always fun, but they were necessary. If I got rewarded for my efforts at all, it wasn't until the end.

Ask yourself: do I have the ability to see them through to completion? You won't be able to finish everything you start. But if you can, you should.

When I was in Boy Scouts I had intended to reach the rank of Eagle Scout. The only thing I had left was to complete my Eagle Scout Project. Then we moved and I switched schools. The move was hard for me to cope with, and we never found another Boy Scout troop nearby that worked with our schedule. I never did finish. While it was disappointing and I regret not finishing, it made a big impact on me—not to reach a goal that I was very close to.

The things you complete or accomplish often end up on your resume. You may be asked to discuss them with other people so that they can learn from your experience. Not everyone can stick with something for the long term. By learning how to do so, you set yourself apart from the majority of people.

Good Work Values

Having good work values encompasses everything else that goes into having a good work ethic. A good work ethic is a vague term that covers everything else listed above and then some.

A lot of the values that go into work ethic are intangible (meaning they aren't physical and can't be touched) because they have to do with your character. Are you honest and responsible? Are you reliable and dedicated? Can you work well with your team? Are you professional and respectful? Are you someone that you would want to work with? Do you deliver quality work and have an eye for detail? Do you keep your promises?

Good work values are reflected in your personal life. If you are an honest, caring, and committed person, these values will show up in your workplace. The interpersonal skills[5] you use among family and friends will help make you successful at work.

Some interpersonal skills can be learned and applied to both personal and professional settings. I use a lot of tools I learned about body language to get to know people better in both settings. Luckily for me, the core of my character is to be honest and kind, which is the foundation that I built off of when developing my interpersonal skills.

While interpersonal skills vary for everyone, depending on personality and strengths, the core of it is to be the type of person that you would want working for you.

Have an Entrepreneurial Mindset

Once you've established your place in a job, this mindset will take you to the next level. Try to get inside the head of your boss and predict what they are going to ask of you and of the company. Look for flaws, shortcomings, and opportunities to come up with solutions for them. This problem-solving mentality is called having an entrepreneurial mindset.

When a problem is presented by your boss in a meeting, be willing to give

---

[5] Interpersonal skills are behaviors and qualities you have or can develop that help you interact with other people. This can include listening, teamwork, leadership, patience, and more.

your own opinion. You may be wrong, but you should be willing to speak up. The feedback you get on your idea will help you learn and grow. It also shows your boss that you have an interest in helping the organization succeed.

If an opportunity comes up to work on a special task force, you should volunteer to participate. At the very least, you will learn a lot more about the company. But you will also learn about other members of the task force and get an idea of what direction the company is headed in the future.

Developing an entrepreneurial mindset will help you in an organization and will also help you should you choose to ever start your own business. If you've practiced the skills of an entrepreneur while working for someone else, you will be that much more prepared if you do decide to go out on your own.

Why I Want My Daughter to Know This

When my daughter enters the workforce, she will have more skills and experience than most. Ashla has more content for her resume than I did when I was her age (currently fourteen) since she has already worked as a babysitter, gotten her junior black belt in karate, and consistently volunteered with several organizations.

These things will get her in the door, but it is the principles in this chapter that will help her succeed at any job.

Referring to the first chapter, these principles help winners win. You need to have the right mindset and mental tools before you can succeed. The rest of the information in this book is near useless if you can't first earn money. That's why I spent two chapters in a book about money, first talking about mentality.

3: FIRST JOB

"So how do you actually get a job? Do you just walk into a business and ask them for one?" Ashla asked me one day.

"Pretty much…"

Before I could continue, she asked, "But how do you know if they are hiring?"

"Sometimes they have a sign up in a window, outside, or inside by a cash register. You just have to pay attention and see…"

"So only people that have those signs are hiring?"

"No, those places are more open to people, but a lot of places may be hiring and not put up those signs. A few years ago, they purposefully didn't put up signs because there were so many people looking for work that businesses didn't want to be overwhelmed with job seekers. At the ice cream shop I worked at back then, we went to online-only applications because we were going through so much paper and ink printing applications at a time when we were not even considering hiring people."

"So, you can apply online?"

"For many places, yes. But there are just as many places that you can't. The best way to find out if a business is hiring and how to apply is to go in and ask them. When you do, make sure you look nice and are respectful. And try to avoid times when those businesses are really busy. Like at the ice cream store, if someone asked for an application when we were really busy during the evening rush, we told them we weren't hiring."

"What if they could have been a great worker?"

"How could they be? They didn't take time to look around and see that we had more important things we were working on. Chances are good if we hired them, they would struggle because they couldn't tell what tasks were most important at any time."

"So you want to make a good impression before you even get to the interview," Ashla stated.

There are countless books, websites, and other resources you can turn to for great advice on applying for jobs, making a good first impression, and interviewing well. I'll touch on some basics here, because basic techniques will help you get a job and start earning money. This book's focus is on money topics, so I'll share some insights on money issues at a first job.

Applying for a Job

As I said in the chapter introduction, you need to present yourself as well as you can from the very beginning. Before you even start applying, make sure you are ready for what will happen when they call you. Build an appropriate resume that highlights your strengths; practice your interview skills, including clearly stating why you want the job; identify your weaknesses; be prepared to check your email daily, including your junk mail; and know your interview and work availability. Lastly, check your attitude. If you go into looking for a job with the attitude of "they owe me a job," you will struggle to find one or find a job that is a bad fit. If you go into looking for a job with the attitude of "I want to show them how great of an employee I am going to be," you will be more successful in finding a job that is a good fit.

As you progress through your life, you will likely be asked for a resume instead of, or in addition to, completing an application. A resume has a lot of the same information that an application asks for. When you get to the point of needing a resume, check online for examples of high-quality resumes. A resume will have your name and contact information at the top; often an objective line where you state your job search intention; then your job history complete with job title, employer name, address and phone number; and bulleted descriptions of what you did while you were working there. Additional information that can go onto a resume includes volunteer experience and any clubs and sports you participated in. If you held a position of authority (like club treasurer or team captain), that should go on the resume as well. You can list awards you've won and describe what it took to win them. You can list skills you have developed. These can be hard skills like knowing a certain computer program, or soft skills like teamwork or communication. If the skill sounds vague, make sure you describe what you are good at. Rather than saying "good communicator," say "skilled in both verbal and written communication as demonstrated by work performed at XYZ corporation." If you don't have any of these—get some (see chapter 1 on change in mindset). When creating your resume, it is important to be a professional *you*. So let your resume reflect your personality a little. Lastly, you can list references on your resume. If your resume looks a little empty, this is a good way to fill it up. If your resume is already filled, you should have a separate page with reference information on it, so it is readily available. You should notify your references before you start applying to give them a heads-up that you are looking for employment so they are not caught off guard if the employer follows up with them.

Many employers see an empty resume (or an empty application) as a lack of experience. Do your best to fill the page with quality content that highlights your best work. Resumes are hard because it feels like you're bragging about yourself. But a resume is a quick snapshot of who you are and what you have done, so take the time to showcase yourself and give yourself a great shot at getting an interview and possibly the job.

An application is concerned with much of the same information, but the resume allows you the opportunity to describe what you did for the company and let others know what skills you've developed as a result. The resume is a great way to help the employer remember who you are and give them more information than what may be asked on their application.

Don't lie on a resume or an application. In the interview, you will likely be asked questions about what you've put down. Be prepared to talk about anything on your resume.

When you start applying for jobs, always make sure you have printed copies of your resume with you. This can be used as a guide when filling out any application, and it shows the employer you did something to prepare for work.

If you are inquiring about open positions in person, make sure you have nice, clean clothes on. Since most first jobs are service oriented (like restaurants and stores), they usually have fairly standard dress code policies that limit what their employees can wear. Typically, this includes closed-toed shoes (no sandals), long pants (no shirts or skirts), and a collared shirt (like a polo or a button-down shirt). If you go out job seeking in a similar outfit, it is easier for people to see you as a potential employee because you already look the part.

Be respectful of the employees that are working when you go in to apply. If they are busy, wait for your turn patiently. Allow them to help customers before assisting you (within reason). If they are really busy, you may want to come back at a different time. Some of these employees may participate in hiring decisions, training, or be your supervisor if you are hired. It shows that you understand their business enough to come back during a more appropriate time so they can focus on their current guests.

If they give you a paper application to fill out, it may be best to fill it out right there and turn it in. If a business really needs help, they may interview you right then—especially, if you come in dressed the part. This is also why you should have your resume handy. A paper application looks much stronger when it is accompanied with a resume. Even if you have your resume, make sure you fill out the paper application completely. Do not put "see resume" on their paper application, because they will likely tell you to "see other employment." Completing their application shows that you want to take the time to follow the rules and expectations, not cut corners. If you take the application with you to fill out, make sure you take it back to turn it in at a time when the business is not as busy.

Applications for different businesses ask for a lot of the same information. I found it easier to keep a pre-filled-out application with me when I went around applying for jobs so I had addresses and phone numbers for references and dates of any activities that I had participated in. Most of this information should be found on your completed resume also, so you need to determine a system that works for you. Not sure what information you need? Look up "application" online, and you will find many samples to help you feel prepared.

Have a pen, so you can fill out applications without relying on the business to provide you with one. This demonstrates your being serious and prepared.

There is a good chance you will be directed to a website to complete an application. Make sure you know what the website is, and be thorough about filling out online applications, as some larger companies use computer programs to sift through large numbers of online applications. The more complete yours is the better chance you will have of making it past the computer program. Again, do not put "see resume" on any part of their application, even if the resume is included. Do the work to get the job to show them you will do the work in the job.

Some other notes on applying for a job: make sure your phone voicemail is appropriate. When my daughter first started asking about jobs, I noticed that her phone voicemail was from a few years earlier when she sounded very young in it. It could be a turnoff for employers if they are hoping for more mature people to have someone have a voicemail that sounds like a young child or is immature/inappropriate. Even the silly voicemails like "Hello, hello, oh wait this is my voicemail. Leave a message" can be a turn-off for employers.

For the same reason, you should also clean up your social media. Update your profile pictures so that you represent your best self. Delete posts if you used bad language or posted potentially offensive material. More and more employers are checking this stuff out before they hire you. They like to know how you will represent their company if they hire you, and this is part of looking your best.

The Interview

Arrive prepared and arrive early. Remember, your interview begins the moment you enter the parking lot. My wife works with youth to assist them in getting jobs, and she had a client who "aced" the interview but lost the job. While he was in the parking lot before the interview, he cussed at a customer, and a cart attendant saw this and reported to the hiring manager, "Don't hire him, he does not care about our customers." Typically, I arrive fifteen minutes early to every interview. I want to show them that I respected their time. Arriving early is also a way to show your potential employer that you won't be late when you are working for them.

Arriving prepared also means showing up dressed well. Look at how their employees are dressed and take it up a notch. You don't need to wear a suit and tie to every job, but you should try to look like you belong.

I always brought a copy of reference information with me in case they didn't ask for references on the application. A reference is a person that the person hiring can contact to get more information about you. The reference should know about your work habits and personality. Friends and family are not good references. Your teacher can be a good reference but will probably hesitate to share their personal phone number with you. If you have done volunteering, the people in charge of that would be good references. Other good references would be from your place of worship or coaches from sports you participate in.

If you can, it is best to get references from a variety of sources—not just all teachers or place-of-worship members. You should include their name, professional title, and either personal or professional phone number, email and address. You get all this information to be thorough and show that they really do know you. You should always ask a reference ahead of time whether you can use them as a reference. That way they are prepared if someone contacts them. If someone is not comfortable being a reference for you—don't force it. They probably won't be a good one anyway.

You should understand your own schedule so that you can communicate it to the employer. If you are going to be working around a school schedule or other activities, you need to know what those time restrictions are, keeping in mind transportation needs. If this is a summer job and your time availability will change when you go back to school, you need to let them know that.

Other ways to show up for an interview prepared is to have researched the company you are applying for. You should have a basic understanding of how their business works. Do a quick internet search and see whether there have been any recent news articles about them. You should also check out their website. Great things to look for is their mission statement and "messages" to the customers. Pay attention to products they sell or promote, etc. If you've been into their business before, what did you notice about their employees? Were they friendly, hard working, always smiling, passionate about their job, etc. How can you fit in?

At the interview, give a firm handshake when you are first introduced and at the end. Sit up straight and maintain eye contact. If eye contact is hard for you, look at their nose or forehead between their eyes. Avoid using slang words or filler words such as "like" or "um." Remember to breathe and take your time thinking of what you want to say. A few seconds pause shows that you want to consider their question before answering.

Be prepared to talk about yourself. One of the first questions employers ask have something to do with "tell me a little about yourself." This can be one of the hardest questions, especially if you're nervous. Practice! Talk about your work habits when it comes to school, volunteering, or participating in sports and activities. They may ask you about your activities, so feel free to talk about them more. You should be able to describe in detail what you did and even be willing to share a story about your experience if you think it is relevant. If you don't share, you may have missed an opportunity to show them a valuable part of who you are as a worker. Brag a little—don't be cocky, but they don't know you, and this is your chance to showcase your best self.

Other things to keep in mind—what are your strengths? Know how to talk about weaknesses, and include ways to overcome them. Telling an employer "I'm not great at managing my time" doesn't represent you in a good light. Instead tell them, "I get really invested in projects and could work on them all day, but ensure I set timers for myself to keep on track with other things that need to be done." This shows that you have a weakness, but you also have a way to overcome it. Remind yourself what your top skills are and how you can represent that best to the employer. I highly recommend practicing your interview skills before the interview.

Always have a couple of questions to ask the interviewer. This shows that you can think things through (critical thinking) and that you are serious. It's best to write these down before the interview and reference them if you need to. An employer would rather you pull out a list of questions than say "I had some, but I forgot." Stay away from things like "how much vacation do I get" or "what does this job pay?" It gives the wrong impression to the employer about the reasons you're applying—especially if it's your fist job. Some of my favorite questions are the following:

- What do you think would make someone successful in this position?
- Why is this position available? Why did the last person leave?
- What does the training for this position look like?
- If hired, whom will I report to?
- Is there anything you would like to know about me that I haven't answered?
- When do you expect to make a hiring decision?

Employers like hiring people who seem invested in the job. These questions can help illustrate that.

After the interview, follow up. This can be the most important part of the interview if they are on the fence of whom to hire. Send a three-sentence email thanking them for the interview, listing one thing you loved learning about the position, and inviting them to reach out with any other questions. If they said they would let you know by Thursday, call back on Friday to check in (keep in mind to do this when they are not busy). No matter what their decision, always thank them for their time and the opportunity to interview. They may be calling you if the other person they chose turns out to be a bad fit.

The Paperwork

The first day you show up for a job the employer will require you to fill out some paperwork. Each business is different and may have safety documents, employee handbooks, or rules and regulation documents for you to sign. I recommend reading through anything the employer gives you to better understand their expectations. Your employer may also request that you fill out a direct deposit form, but Form W-4 and Form I-9 are required by the government and will always need to be completed. These forms will require identification from you. The most common documents are state-issued ID (such as a driver's license) and your Social Security card. Some other forms of identification may be substituted, such as a passport, original birth certificate, or school ID card. I recommend asking your employer when they call to ensure you have proper documentation. You cannot start working until they have all the proper documentation and it is processed into their system.

Form W-4, Employee's Wage Withholding Certificate helps you determine how much tax you should have withheld from your paycheck each pay-period. This money is then sent directly to the government on your behalf. Employers are not legally allowed to recommend how to fill out these forms, so if you're unsure, talk to someone trusted in your family for advice.

Step 1 asks for information so they can identify whom the form is for. You will need your Social Security number (conveniently found on the card your employer asked you for). Form W-4 will also ask for your name and address as well as your tax-filing status. If it is your first job, there is a high likelihood that you aren't married. If you never have been, you'll mark the *single* box.

Step 2 applies to you only if you have multiple jobs or are married with a spouse that works.

Step 3 applies to you only if you have children.

Step 4 needs to be completed only if you want extra taxes withheld. I have had extra taxes withheld only when I had other income from rentals, which wasn't being automatically taxed. It helped me pay taxes throughout the year for that added income rather than try to remember to write the IRS a check for rental income.

Step 5 requires you to sign and date it. Everything after this (a couple of pages not shown here) is for your new employer to complete.

For more information on taxes, see chapter 8.

FIRST JOB

Form W-4

Department of the Treasury
Internal Revenue Service

Employee's Withholding Certificate

► Complete Form W-4 so that your employer can withhold the correct federal income tax from your pay.
► Give Form W-4 to your employer.
► Your withholding is subject to review by the IRS.

OMB No. 1545-0074

2020

Step 1: Enter Personal Information	(a) First name and middle initial	Last name	(b) Social security number

Address

City or town, state, and ZIP code

► Does your name match the name on your social security card? If not, to ensure you get credit for your earnings, contact SSA at 800-772-1213 or go to www.ssa.gov.

(c) ☐ Single or Married filing separately
☐ Married filing jointly (or Qualifying widow(er))
☐ Head of household (Check only if you're unmarried and pay more than half the costs of keeping up a home for yourself and a qualifying individual.)

Complete Steps 2–4 ONLY if they apply to you; otherwise, skip to Step 5. See page 2 for more information on each step, who can claim exemption from withholding, when to use the online estimator, and privacy.

Step 2: Multiple Jobs or Spouse Works

Complete this step if you (1) hold more than one job at a time, or (2) are married filing jointly and your spouse also works. The correct amount of withholding depends on income earned from all of these jobs.

Do **only one** of the following.

(a) Use the estimator at www.irs.gov/W4App for most accurate withholding for this step (and Steps 3–4); **or**

(b) Use the Multiple Jobs Worksheet on page 3 and enter the result in Step 4(c) below for roughly accurate withholding; **or**

(c) If there are only two jobs total, you may check this box. Do the same on Form W-4 for the other job. This option is accurate for jobs with similar pay; otherwise, more tax than necessary may be withheld . . . . . . ► ☐

TIP: To be accurate, submit a 2020 Form W-4 for all other jobs. If you (or your spouse) have self-employment income, including as an independent contractor, use the estimator.

Complete Steps 3–4(b) on Form W-4 for only ONE of these jobs. Leave those steps blank for the other jobs. (Your withholding will be most accurate if you complete Steps 3–4(b) on the Form W-4 for the highest paying job.)

Step 3: Claim Dependents

If your income will be $200,000 or less ($400,000 or less if married filing jointly):

Multiply the number of qualifying children under age 17 by $2,000 ► $ _____

Multiply the number of other dependents by $500 . . . . ► $ _____

Add the amounts above and enter the total here . . . . | 3 | $

Step 4 (optional): Other Adjustments

(a) **Other income (not from jobs).** If you want tax withheld for other income you expect this year that won't have withholding, enter the amount of other income here. This may include interest, dividends, and retirement income . . . . | 4(a) | $

(b) **Deductions.** If you expect to claim deductions other than the standard deduction and want to reduce your withholding, use the Deductions Worksheet on page 3 and enter the result here . . . . | 4(b) | $

(c) **Extra withholding.** Enter any additional tax you want withheld each **pay period** . | 4(c) | $

Step 5: Sign Here

Under penalties of perjury, I declare that this certificate, to the best of my knowledge and belief, is true, correct, and complete.

► _____
Employee's signature (This form is not valid unless you sign it.)

► _____
Date

Employers Only	Employer's name and address	First date of employment	Employer identification number (EIN)

For Privacy Act and Paperwork Reduction Act Notice, see page 3.   Cat. No. 10220Q   Form **W-4** (2020)

Form I-9, Employment Eligibility Verification is the second form required by the government, which your employer will have you fill out. This is used to help verify your identity and your right to work in the United States. It requires the same information from you as the previous form but also asks about your residency (whether you are a citizen of the U.S. or have gone through the process to attain proper documentation to work if you are a non-citizen).

Employment Eligibility Verification
Department of Homeland Security
U.S. Citizenship and Immigration Services

USCIS
Form I-9
OMB No. 1615-0047
Expires 10/31/2022

▶ START HERE: Read instructions carefully before completing this form. The instructions must be available, either in paper or electronically, during completion of this form. Employers are liable for errors in the completion of this form.

ANTI-DISCRIMINATION NOTICE: It is illegal to discriminate against work-authorized individuals. Employers CANNOT specify which document(s) an employee may present to establish employment authorization and identity. The refusal to hire or continue to employ an individual because the documentation presented has a future expiration date may also constitute illegal discrimination.

Section 1. Employee Information and Attestation *(Employees must complete and sign Section 1 of Form I-9 no later than the first day of employment, but not before accepting a job offer.)*

Last Name (Family Name)	First Name (Given Name)	Middle Initial	Other Last Names Used (if any)

Address (Street Number and Name)	Apt. Number	City or Town	State	ZIP Code

Date of Birth (mm/dd/yyyy)	U.S. Social Security Number	Employee's E-mail Address	Employee's Telephone Number

I am aware that federal law provides for imprisonment and/or fines for false statements or use of false documents in connection with the completion of this form.

I attest, under penalty of perjury, that I am (check one of the following boxes):

☐ 1. A citizen of the United States

☐ 2. A noncitizen national of the United States *(See instructions)*

☐ 3. A lawful permanent resident   (Alien Registration Number/USCIS Number)

☐ 4. An alien authorized to work   until (expiration date, if applicable, mm/dd/yyyy).
Some aliens may write "N/A" in the expiration date field. *(See instructions)*

Aliens authorized to work must provide only one of the following document numbers to complete Form I-9.
An Alien Registration Number/USCIS Number OR Form I-94 Admission Number OR Foreign Passport Number.

QR Code - Section 1
Do Not Write In This Space

1. Alien Registration Number/USCIS Number: _____
   OR
2. Form I-94 Admission Number: _____
   OR
3. Foreign Passport Number: _____
   Country of Issuance: _____

Signature of Employee	Today's Date (mm/dd/yyyy)

Preparer and/or Translator Certification (check one):
☐ I did not use a preparer or translator.   ☐ A preparer(s) and/or translator(s) assisted the employee in completing Section 1.
(Fields below must be completed and signed when preparers and/or translators assist an employee in completing Section 1.)
I attest, under penalty of perjury, that I have assisted in the completion of Section 1 of this form and that to the best of my knowledge the information is true and correct.

Signature of Preparer or Translator	Today's Date (mm/dd/yyyy)

Last Name (Family Name)	First Name (Given Name)

Address (Street Number and Name)	City or Town	State	ZIP Code

🛑 *Employer Completes Next Page* 🛑

Your employer may also ask you to fill out a direct deposit form. Direct deposit allows your employer to put your paycheck directly into your account. This will be deposited whenever the employer normally pays its employees. Each job has different pay periods, so if you're unsure, ask your employer. It is most common to get paid bi-weekly (every other week) or at the end of the month.

A direct deposit form will require bank information from you (see chapter 4). There is not a standard form that I can show you. At a minimum, the form will ask you for your name, your bank's name, the bank's routing number (nine digits listed first on the very bottom of a check), and your account number (next set of ten digits). If you don't know where to find this information, ask your bank and they will guide you or provide you with their own form that you can give to the employer. The direct deposit form will then ask for your signature, which authorizes the employer to deposit your paycheck automatically rather than give you an actual check.

At the time of payroll, whether you get a paper check or direct deposit, your employer will give you a paystub (see chapter 4). A paystub shows you how many hours you worked, what your rate of pay is (make sure these are both correct), what was withheld for payroll taxes, and what you receive as your net pay. Net pay is the money you get after any withholdings. For your first job, your only withholdings will likely be for taxes, but the employer may also hold some back if you have joined an employer-sponsored health insurance plan that you have to pay towards or if you decide to contribute to a company 401k plan (both of these are discussed later in the book).

The most important part about being a new employee is asking questions. So if you need guidance, advocate for yourself and ask your employer to help you. They have probably dealt with this before.

Why I Want My Daughter to Know This

Entire books have been written on interview techniques. Numerous resources for preparing your best application and resume are available online. Yet many young people don't know about their existence or chose not to get acquainted with them.

I didn't know about such resources when I was looking for my first few jobs. I applied for a movie theater and never heard back. Then an ice cream store and was hired on the spot after a quick chat. When I went looking for my second job, I applied at a restaurant, which also hired me then and there. So getting a job appeared to be pretty easy. Of course, it was just good timing.

A few years later, the economy changed, and it got much harder to find a job. For months, I was doing what I had always done to look for work but wasn't getting a call back from anywhere. So, I spent some time reading books on interviewing, resumes, and applications and eventually did find a job. This also helped me later when I started applying for jobs that were in much more professional environments.

Thanks to my research, I (1) secured an interview by having a great resume, (2) used some techniques to appear more likeable during the interview by means of demonstrating my intelligence, and (3) followed up with the company.

Of course, the entry-level position interviews and application process are vastly different from those for a position of a company's vice president. Still, in either situation, you want to appear intelligent, skilled, and likeable.

4: BANKS

"Dad, what type of account do I need to have to get a debit card?"
"A checking account allows you to have a debit card and also checks."
"What do you use checks for?"
"I use them a lot when paying people from our business accounts. Old people used to use them a lot to pay for everything. You will probably only use a check to pay for rent."
"So what's the difference between a checking and a savings account?"

Once you've got a job, you're going to need somewhere to put the money you are earning. Whether you know it yet or not, life is a lot easier if you have a bank account where you can manage your bills from. Hence, this chapter on banks.

There are two primary types of personal bank accounts: checking and savings. Beyond that, there are also Certificates of Deposit (CDs) and Money Market Accounts.

Savings Accounts

Once my daughter started babysitting and earning her own money, we opened up a savings account for her. After many discussions about money and handling it correctly, we decided to start her with a savings account that she could draw the money out of without needing my wife or me present. This gave her a bunch of freedom that she thought was cool. It was also a relatively safe way for her to learn the basics of handling her own money.

The only way for her to access her money was to go to the bank and pull it out herself. She was able to put her cash in there and earn a little bit of interest on it as well as put in any checks she received for birthdays. Not using debit cards and checks protected her from overdrawing the account.

The bank we chose was directly across the street from her school, so she could easily go by after school to pull out some cash if she wanted to grab coffee with her friends. Also, there were no monthly fees or minimums she had to keep in there. My wife and I were also both on the account and could monitor what she was doing and easily put money into the account if she had a specific need we agreed to help with. It was a very safe way for her to begin learning how to handle a bank account.

Savings accounts have some specific rules that we discussed with her and I am sharing here:

- Unlimited deposits: Put in as much money as often as you want.
- Six withdrawals per quarter (unless done in person): This is a Federal regulation, and they typically give you a warning the first time if you exceed the limit. Typically, if you exceed it more than once, the bank will close your account and mail you a check with any remaining balance.
- Most of the time, electronic transfers and payments do not count against the rule of six, meaning you can go online and transfer money to a different account or set up recurring ACH/EFT[6] payments for bills such as a cell phone or utilities.
- Minimal interest: You can earn some interest, but it is not much when compared to other accounts such as CDs.
- Beware of monthly minimums: Some banks will charge you a service fee if you fall below a certain amount. If you think you will consistently have this problem, it may be better to have a checking account with no checks or debit cards, as you won't be earning much interest and checking accounts are less likely to have service charges.
- Eliminate paper statement charges: If your bank charges for paper statements, make sure you get set up for electronic statements. It eliminates clutter in your life and saves you money.

---

[6] ACH stands for Automated Clearing House, and EFT stands for Electronic Funds Transfer. The terms are often used interchangeably by bankers. The difference is that an EFT is a broader term that covers all electronic payments, whereas an ACH is a specific type of transfer done from bank to bank and grouped together in batches. When an employer pays all of their employees at once electronically, it is usually through an ACH. EFTs include ACHs, wire transfers (explained later in this chapter), and electronic check processing (like mobile deposit, also explained later).

Checking Accounts

As of right now, my daughter doesn't have a checking account. Having been in banking, I saw many people who were inexperienced handling money get in trouble with debit cards. Checks weren't really an issue for them, as they have grown up in a world where checks are almost completely unnecessary.

Checks start becoming an issue once young people get a little older and move out on their own. They write a check for their rent, and it takes a couple of days for it to come out of their account. For a few days, they have money in their account, and they use their debit card for lunch, coffee, shopping at Target, etc. Then the check hits, and either it is returned without being paid or it overdraws their account.

Overdrawing an account means that the bank pays the check, even though there is not enough money in the account. Effectively, the bank lends you the difference, because they have faith that you will bring in more money to repay them. They don't do this for free, as it is a risk for the bank, and typically charge you an overdraft fee. Now you have to pay back however much they lent you and then some before your account has money in it again. Also, if you let your account sit overdrawn for too long, the bank will start charging you a recurring overdraft fee every day.

Bouncing a check means the check is returned because there are not sufficient funds[7] in the account to pay it. The bank charges you a non-sufficient funds fee (similar to the overdraft fee), because you put them in a hard spot. The check gets returned to the bank account of the person you wrote it to. Typically, that person gets charged a fee in their bank account, and now they are really angry at you. Your check was no good, and now you've cost them money as well. They will probably expect you to pay them back for the cost of the bounced check on their end.

Back in the day, old people would write checks without any money in their account and expect them to "float." Meaning they knew they were getting paid on the first of the month so they would write a check on the 25th of the prior month and mail it. It would spend a few days in the mail, and then it would get to the person they were paying. That person may take a day or two to deposit it into their bank. Then it could take up to seven days for their bank to successfully get the money from your bank. So, the check could "float" with no money in the account it was written on for almost two weeks.

---

[7] *Non-Sufficient Funds (NSF)* means there is not enough money in the account.

Unfortunately, some old people still do this, but banks have gotten faster (and the mail has too). A check dropped in the mail today could be at its destination in two days. The person receiving your check can immediately deposit it in their bank via either a mobile deposit (taking a picture of it with their phone) or Remote Deposit Capture (where they have a specialized machine attached to their computer, which scans the check to the bank immediately). The bank receives it and sends it to your bank electronically in the same instant. There is now a draw on your account for that check in as little as two days, compared to the previous two weeks. So old people are just as likely to overdraw their account as young people. The best way to prevent overdrawing your account is to keep a cushion in it of extra money or sign up for an overdraft protection service (discussed later in this chapter).

Here are the features of typical checking accounts:

- Debit cards: These allow instant access to the funds in your checking account to allow you to pay for things. The bank will allow you to overdraw your account with a debit card (they want the fees).
- Checks: The old way of paying. They come in books and need to be filled out properly to be used. Here are some tips for the best way to fill out a check:
  - "Pay to the Order of" Line: Write the name of the person or company you are paying here. NEVER LEAVE IT BLANK if you have filled out everything else. If you do leave it blank and it gets lost, anyone that finds it can write their name on that line and get the money for it. You can write "Cash" on it if you are presenting it at the bank to withdraw cash from your account, but this is just as bad as leaving it blank. If you are withdrawing money, it is safest to write your own name on the check.
  - "$" Box: Use numbers to write how much you want to pay.
  - Line followed by "Dollars": You need to spell out the dollar amount you want to pay. This is the legal amount that the check can be exchanged for cash. If this is different from the "$" box, the bank will default to this line. It is best to write this out in cursive, as it is harder to alter. Use the word "and" only between the dollar amount and the cents. If you do not use the whole space, draw a line down the middle of any remaining space to show that you purposefully left it blank. You can write numbers for cents, but show it as a

fraction out of 100. For example, if I were writing the amount $1,234.50, I would write it as such:

- *One thousand two hundred thirty-four and 50/100*

o "For" or "Memo" Line: This line doesn't affect the check but is for your use to identify what you are paying for. In the event you need to look back at the check, this helps you remember what the check was for.

o Signature Line ending in "MP": Sign your name (typically in cursive) here to agree to everything you've put on the check.

Check Example

```
                                                               123
John Smith
1234 Main Street                              DATE _____
Anytown, NY 12345

PAY TO THE                                              $ [          ]
ORDER OF    _____
            _____   DOLLARS

FIRST BANK OF USA
6789 2ND STREET
ANYTOWN, NY 12345
                                                               MP
MEMO   _____    _____

I: 123456789 I: 1223334444 "I  0123
```

Since we are on the subject of checks, it's important to know what you need to do to accept checks. When you accept a check from someone and take it to your bank to deposit it, on the back of the check you will need to endorse it. *Endorsing* it means signing your name on it as a sort of verification that you are receiving the funds. You should always endorse a check the way it is spelled on the front. For me, this sometimes means signing "Josh Fulenwider" instead of "Joshua Fulenwider." But this can also include misspellings, e.g., "Fullenwider" vs. "Fulenwider." Oftentimes, if there is a misspelling, the bank will ask that you sign it the way it is made out on the front and then again with your correct name.

Once you've endorsed a check, you can do a couple of things to it. First, you can write "For Deposit Only" on it, which means it can't be cashed and can go into only your account. You can further specify—"For Deposit Only Account ########." By adding your specific account on it, you are telling the bank which account you want it to go into. Make sure you get your account number right!

Second, you can add a "Pay to the Order of (New Person)." Writing this on the back of your check makes the check legally payable to the new person. That person can then take the check and either deposit it or cash it. Because this is easy to write on the back of a check that is either found or stolen by someone else, you shouldn't endorse a check until you are ready to deposit it either in person at a bank or via a mobile app.

Lastly, you can write "For Mobile Deposit Only" beneath the endorsement if you are depositing it via a mobile app. This limits what can be done with the check to only a mobile deposit. Some banks may require that you add their bank name to this as well so that you can't deposit the check into several banks.

Overdraft Protection

Overdraft protection is a product that banks sometimes offer. It typically requires either a credit check or a history of good account management with the bank (meaning few if any overdrafts and timely repayment). Essentially, on a personal account, a bank makes available $500 to $1,000 credit line that can be drawn on in the event you draw past your account balance. This prevents you from getting hit with expensive overdraft or non-sufficient funds fees, including the recurring fees. This is structured similar to a credit card in that there is usually a high interest rate, and it requires a minimum monthly payment that includes all interest and some principal repayment (see the definition of principal and interest in chapter 7 on loans). You can pay the remaining balance of the line back at any time and do not need to wait for the monthly payment to be due.

In addition to protecting you from high fees, overdraft protection also ensures that you don't have any "bounced" checks or returned automatic payments (see chapter 5 on managing your bills). This is helpful in that many places will charge you if you bounce a check made out to them. For example, if you had written a check for $100 to Bob's Plumbing, and it gets returned (bounces), Bob calls you up and demands the $100 plus a fee for the problem. These vary, but commonly it is around $20.

I have seen overdraft protection lines structured in two different ways. Some banks just attach it to the existing checking account, making it all one product. This makes it very easy to repay the line, because as soon as you put a deposit in, it will pay back all the money owed. More commonly, I have seen it set up as a separate account, which adds a step to repayment—you have to deposit money and then transfer money over to repay the credit line. The difference between these two setups can be seen in either online or mobile banking. When logging in, you will see either one or two accounts, depending on the structure.

CDs

A CD is not a disc that has music on it. CD stands for Certificate of Deposit. They were named that because back in the day you received a certificate, typically green, that told you what you had deposited into your CD and the basic terms of the CD.

CDs earn a higher interest rate than savings accounts do, but the money is locked up for specified periods of time. Most of the time, the longer you agree to keep the money in the CD the higher the interest rate you will receive on it. CDs can be as short as one month, but many banks will not make them for less than three months, and some won't even go less than a year. The most common terms they are set up for are one year, eighteen months, three years, and five years.

If you have extra money, they are a decent way to earn a bit more in interest than you would if you had just put it into a typical savings account, however, they don't earn as much as you could if you were to invest in the stock market. They are good for saving up for mid-term large purchases. Saving up for a home would be a good example of this. You can put money steadily into CDs for several years with the intention that in five years you are going to buy a home. You would structure your CDs so that they all "mature" at the same time in five years, giving you access to the money when you are planning on using it.

This money is not subject to market fluctuations (see chapter 16 on choosing investments in your retirement accounts), so you don't have to worry about there being a down market when you want to draw the money out. However, if you need the money for something prior to their maturity, you can draw it out, but you will likely be facing early withdrawal penalties, which can erase some or all of the interest you've earned up until that point and possibly some of the principal as well.

Money Market Accounts

Money market accounts are designed to take the highlights of checking and savings accounts. They earn interest but also allow some limited check writing. The downside to them is that they typically require higher opening deposits and higher required minimum balances. You cannot substitute one for your checking account, because you are limited on the number of transactions per month. Due to the downsides of money market accounts, I didn't see them used a lot when I was in banking. With the introduction of Internet and mobile banking, it has been just as easy to have a checking account and a savings account. Thus when you need more money in checking, you can just transfer it from your savings account (assuming you have money in there!).

I feel like I should add more about money market accounts, but they aren't that common anymore, as there just isn't much demand for them.

What Is Interest?

I used to be in banking but then I lost interest! (excuse the lame joke).

Interest is money paid on borrowed money. This is the cost of borrowing that money. Banks pay you interest when you keep money in their bank, because they are borrowing that money from you. You pay the bank interest when you have to borrow money from them in the form of a loan. To be profitable, banks try to pay you as little interest as possible while getting as much interest as they can on loans.

It's in your best interest (pun intended) to shop around for both deposit accounts and loans. Maximize what you receive on your savings account while minimizing what you pay on any loan you take out.

Banks have other fees that they charge, so this isn't the only thing to look at, but it is a good first step to take when comparing products at different banks.

Other Bank Products

- Mobile banking: You can do so much from your phone now. A bank with a good app will allow you to check account balances, view your transaction history, look up check images, transfer money between accounts, deposit a check by taking a picture of it, and pay other people.

- Online banking: Before the rise of mobile apps, online banking was one of the biggest breakthroughs in banking in recent years. It allowed you to do most of the things a mobile app would do, except paying people was a little more cumbersome through a feature called bill pay, and the only people that could deposit checks online were usually business owners that were specifically set up for it.

- Bill pay: I mentioned it before. This feature lets you pay people who may not be set up to take other forms of payment electronically. Sometimes if a vendor (company) is set up, they can take electronic payments through bill pay. Otherwise, the bank will print and mail a physical check to the vendor. This is very helpful for payments that happen every month, but the company can't set you up with automatic payments (i.e., rent payments to landlords or some small trash companies).

- Safety deposit boxes: These are boxes locked up inside the bank's vault that only you have the key to. They usually have a low annual cost to them. They are helpful for storing valuables or important documents. I would caution you against storing any passports inside safety deposit boxes. I once worked at a bank where the bank president accidentally broke the lock on the vault. It took a couple weeks for a company to be found and then for them to come out and break into the vault. At least one family missed out on their travel plans because their passports were in the vault. More commonly, people forget that the passports are stored there and remember on Friday evening after the bank is closed, with their flight being on Saturday.

- Cashier's check: A cashier's check (sometimes referred to as a bank check) is a means of payment when the money comes out of the bank's account rather than your personal account. Some companies will require that you pay them this way. To get one, you have to go to the bank, have them take money out of your account and put it in their account, and then issue you the check. The person receiving the check has the assurance that the check will not be returned (bounce). The bank will charge you for this service.

- Money Orders: Similar to cashier's checks, a money order can often be obtained from grocery and convenience stores. You have to take them cash, and they give you a check that is guaranteed payment. Western Union is a well-recognized company, which offers money orders inside of grocery stores.

- Wire transfer: This is a form of an electronic funds transfer (EFT) that allows for a same day transfer of money from one bank to another. These are common to use for large purchases, such as buying a home. Unlike other EFTs that may be cancelled or recalled, money sent by a wire transfer is locked into the receiving bank more permanently. It is very rare that money sent by wire can be recalled by the bank that sent it. Because of this feature, the receiving bank deposits the money into the receiving account the same day and allows that money to be used by the account holder (see below for what it means when a "Hold" is placed on money). Wire transfers usually cost money to do.

- ACH: Automated clearing house is a form of transfer between banks when several transactions (deposits and withdrawals) are grouped in batches. These can sometimes be recalled and therefore a hold (see below) is placed on the money for a couple of days.

What Is a Hold?

A hold is when the bank accepts a deposit into one of your accounts but doesn't give you access to that money for a certain period. Holds can last from just a few days up to almost two weeks. Banks do this most often on checks made out by other people. These are the items most likely to bounce when the other person doesn't have money in their account.

Checks from businesses are less risky to a bank, but holds are still likely to be placed. Direct deposits or other ACHs are even less risky and often don't have any hold at all placed on them, while wires have no risk and, therefore, no hold time is put on them.

The only other type of deposit when the bank does not place a hold is when you deposit cash. The bank is accepting real cash, so they have no risk.

Be aware of holds when you are planning on making payments to others. A hold can cause a check to bounce or a debit card to be rejected.

Every bank has their own rules on holds, and some will waive a hold if you have a good history with the bank or the check you are depositing is from another one of their customers. Some banks even have a no-hold policy. However, banks can change their policies at any time. When banks are struggling either due to the economy or other pressures, their hold policy is likely to change.

Difference between Banks and Credit Unions

A bank is a for-profit company, which uses the deposits made by its customers to make loans that yield them the best returns. Banks are owned by shareholders, either privately by individuals or publicly on the stock market. Often they are governed by a professional board of directors that are compensated for their time. Banks pay taxes on their profits.

A credit union is a non-profit entity, which requires anyone that opens an account or takes out a loan with them to be a member. This requires a minimal buy-in of the entity (typically around $25), which is reflected as an amount that can't be withdrawn from the account without closing it. It is owned by its members, not by shareholders. It holds regular meetings, which members are invited to. It is typically managed by a volunteer board of directors. A lot of credit unions are more conservative in their lending, meaning they like to lend to people with better credit. But they also offer better interest rates, because their goal is to serve their members. Since they are a non-profit, credit unions do not pay taxes on their earnings.

A big difference between the two entities is that many credit unions can not make loans or open accounts to businesses. Therefore, credit unions are great for getting car loans, mortgages, home equity lines of credit (HELOCs), or other personal loans. But if you want to start a business or buy an investment property, you will likely need to talk to a bank.

Why I Want My Daughter to Know This

So many people I've talked to seem to be intimidated by bankers. I want my daughter to be comfortable with banks because banks control the money in the world. If she is comfortable with talking to bankers, she can access the money.

Being aware of the different accounts available at a bank gives you the tools to accomplish your saving goals and to manage your spending habits. Some banks may have hybrid accounts that utilize elements of a couple of different types of accounts, but most of them are driven by the more familiar accounts listed here.

5: MANAGING YOUR MONEY

Ashla came home fired up one day after a field trip.

"What's going on?" I asked. "How was the field trip?"

"They made me spend all my money!" she blurted out. She had gone to a Finance Center that focused on teaching kids about budgeting skills. As part of her Junior Achievement class she was in, she had already been learning and practicing the basics of budgeting. At home, we also talked a lot about money, so she was more aware of it than the average kid. By the time she went on this field trip, she was thirteen and was already babysitting to earn her own money and participating in all the family discussions on our businesses and rentals. She also had her own rental house, which we had bought when she was young to pay for her college one day.

"What do you mean?" I asked.

She quickly summarized how they each were randomly assigned incomes and jobs. She happened to get one of the larger incomes in the group. They were then given basic parameters as to what they needed each month: food, housing, car, savings, etc.

Ashla built a budget in which she purchased a used car for about $5,000, ate ramen for every meal of the day, and got the cheapest studio apartment. She was frustrated because she could have gotten a two-bedroom apartment and a roommate, which would have saved her money, but it wasn't allowed. When she turned in her budget, she was saving over half her income each month. She was told she wasn't spending enough and should be saving only $300 per month. She argued and lost, so she added Spam and a couple of other food options but wasn't willing to budge on the apartment or car. She was told that she was saving too much and it was unrealistic.

Budgeting

Budgeting is one of the most boring and self-limiting activities I can imagine. As an entrepreneur, I develop business budgets all the time. As a commercial lender, I spent a good chunk of my time reviewing budgets put together by other people. But when it comes to a personal budget, my eyes glaze over.

There is no single perfect way to do a budget. There are a lot of different ways to budget, and you have to find one that works for you. The important thing about budgeting is to make sure you don't spend more money than you make and to start saving some money for the future. There are many books available that have suggestions for budgeting. Getting into each method would double the size of this book. The core of each one gets into keeping track of your expenses, so you don't overspend.

My wife and I have essentially lived off a two-account budget system for our entire marriage, and it works because its easy. We fill up the first account with money throughout the month to pay the mortgage payment or rent, utilities, and other bills that come out monthly. These amounts are fairly stable and predictable.

Once that account has enough money in it we start putting money in a second account for variable expenses like food, entertainment, and other fun stuff that we don't have to do. If this account ever touches zero, we stop spending money.

Over time, this approach has been progressing, so we added at least one savings account that has helped us with long-term goals such as buying a house or with unexpected expenses like replacing a refrigerator. We've slowly built up both accounts so we have about $1,000 buffer in each in case we plan poorly one month. We also started using a credit card instead of a second account to earn points. We had already established our normal patterns and could predict our behavior.

One time, early in our marriage, we tried to sit down and write a budget. We fought about things, never had an accurate picture of what we spent on certain extras each month because it would vary, and ultimately gave up. It was easiest just to login to online banking every couple of days and see where we were at and compare that with our planned expenses and what we had spent the previous month on extras.

If you are good at budgeting and like it, then I encourage you to keep doing it. Otherwise, the simplest way to budget is not to spend more than you make each month.

Automatic Bill Pay

One of the stupidest ways to lose money is in late fees. Mortgage, rent, cable, water, etc. These are all bills that will charge you a fee if you make a payment late. Rather than trusting yourself to make a payment online or over the phone every month, just set them up for automatic payments.

Most companies will gladly help you set up automatic payments, because they would rather have you pay on time then to pay late. Yes they make extra money in fees if you pay late, but they would rather have the predictable payment. It goes back to the old saying "a bird in hand is worth two in the bush," meaning that it is better to have a little less now than possibly more in the future.

In addition to avoiding late fees, automatic bill pay can help you preserve your credit score (see chapters 6 and 7 on credit and loans, respectively). The only time automatic bill pay doesn't work is if you have no money in your account, so make sure you keep money in there to pay for things.

How to Balance a Checkbook

Balancing a checkbook is the process of making sure you have recorded all the things you've spent money on and the deposits you've made into the bank.

I haven't balanced a checkbook in years. But I think it is something beneficial to learn, because it gives you a basis for how to manage your money. Balancing a checkbook forces you to look at your checking account once a month and to determine how much money you have.

Back in the day, it was necessary to do, because at any single time you could have had five to twenty checks floating around. You had to record each check in your checkbook register, and then you could quickly do the math to determine how much money you still had in your account. You would then "balance your checkbook" when the paper statement arrived at the end of the month. This would tell you what checks were paid and what checks you had written that were still waiting to be paid, and give you the opportunity to catch any transactions that you forgot to write down in your checkbook register.

Two things have vastly undercut the need to balance a checkbook.

First, the decline in the use of checks. Automatic payments and debit cards have cut down on the need to write checks, since the transactions have become nearly instantaneous. This got combined with the second factor—the invention of Internet banking (and later mobile banking), which has allowed people to check their accounts as often as they'd like to see how much money they have.

Balancing a checkbook, however, is a great way to learn basic accounting skills. If you struggle with managing your money, keeping a checkbook register is a great tool to gain control.

Checkbook Register Example

Check #	Date	Transaction	Description	Withdrawal	Deposit	Balance
	7/8/2020	Bank	Opening Deposit		$600.00	$600.00
1001	7/16/2020	Paint Studio	August Class	$100.00		$500.00
Automatic Deposit	7/16/2020	Paycheck			$1,500.00	$2,000.00
Debit Card	7/19/2020	Movie Theater	Tickets	$16.00		$1,984.00
ATM	7/22/2020		Cash	$40.00		$1,944.00
Auto Pay	7/27/2020	The Phone Company		$23.00		$1,921.00

Saving

In my family, we have several saving priorities.

First, we have enough savings that if we accidentally overspend one month it doesn't hurt us financially in the following month. This is a cushion that we keep in the account, which I referenced earlier. We keep about one month's worth of expenses as extra in our account for peace of mind.

Second, we've built up rainy-day savings. For us, this is about six months of expenses so that in the event both my wife and I aren't working we can realistically survive for six months without income. You may be comfortable with three months, or you may want two years of expenses in this account. It is up to you, but it is another peace-of-mind account. We drew on it when we had to replace the roof on our house, and the deductible was higher than what we had expected.

Third, we had started saving for retirement before we got comfortable in our rainy-day account. Our employers offered to match our contributions, and we figured that in the worse case scenario we could pull the money out early and pay a penalty in order to get access to it (see chapter 16 on retirement investing for more information). The employer match was an instant 100 percent return on our money. By being exposed to stocks, we've also consistently earned returns of about 8–10 percent compared to savings account rates of less than 1 percent. This helped us build up savings and wealth much more quickly.

Fourth, we have savings for large purchases. For example, we saved for a while and then used that money to buy a house. Or we saved in order to go on various vacations. Or to purchase investment properties. If you have several savings goals that you want to save for at once, you may want to have multiple accounts.

Why I Want My Daughter to Know This

Why is it important to manage your money well? I would say that if you want to achieve big financial goals in your life, such as buying a home, starting a business, or retiring in comfort, you need to get a handle on how to spend and to save money as early as possible.

Learning how to handle your finances unlocks a world of possibilities and gives you an advantage when it comes to running a business—whether that business is yours or one you work for. The skills built in managing your own money translate into handling the money of a business or an organization.

When my daughter submitted her budget for her finance class, she had the right idea. She should begin saving as much as possible. You never know what tomorrow will (or won't) bring. Living below your means (spending less than you earn) is the best way to ensure you will have money for tomorrow.

6: CREDIT

"Ashla, have we talked about credit scores in the past?"

"Yes."

"What did we talk about?"

"We talked about what they were…"

"That's helpful…"

Eye roll. "We talked about what a credit score is, what it measures, what affects it, and what you need it for. We talked about it after I came home from JA [Junior Achievement], because we'd been talking about it in class and it was really confusing."

"So what did you learn about it?"

"That you are supposed to pay all your stuff on time, or your credit score will go down. If you don't pay your stuff on time and you have to file bankruptcy, it ruins your credit score."

Credit Score

A credit score is a number between 300 and 850 generated by one of the three credit-reporting agencies (Experian, Equifax, and TransUnion). This number tells people whether you are good with money and how likely you are to repay it if they lend it to you. The higher the number the more likely you are going to repay your debts. In my experience, banks get nervous about lending to anyone below a 680, won't lend to anyone with a score below 600, and reserve their best rates for people above a 750. The lowest score I ever saw in banking was about a 420, and the person had to work to get it that low.

The three credit agencies (sometimes called credit bureaus or companies) guard the way they calculate credit scores, but they all take into account basic rules.

- Past due payments – There are three basic buckets that these fall into: 30–60 days past due, 60–90 days past due, and 90+ days past due. The further behind you get in payments the worse the impact on your score. Also, the more late payments you have reported either across accounts or on a single account the worse the impact on your score.

- Negative events – Bankruptcy, foreclosure, repossession, judgment are all major events that dramatically hurt your score. Oftentimes, banks won't lend to anyone who has had a bankruptcy or foreclosure in the last four years. Recent repossessions are also a major turnoff for banks. Judgments will be approached with caution by banks, and there will likely need to be a written explanation given to the bank.

- Recent inquiries – Having a lot of companies check on your credit in a short period can hurt your credit a little. This can indicate to a bank that your life circumstances are changing or that you are getting a little reckless with accumulating debt. Unfortunately, "recent" can mean as recently as any time in the past twelve months.

- High ratio of balance to limits on revolving accounts – Revolving accounts are those that you can pay back the money borrowed and then take money back out again. Credit cards are the most common type of these accounts. Not having a high ratio of balance to limits means don't keep your credit cards maxed out. Banks like to see that you can manage revolving accounts. If you don't have any more money to draw, you may not be managing your spending well. Sometimes, anything above 65 percent usage on these accounts can impact your credit. Anything over 75 percent will definitely start to impact your credit.

- Absence of trade lines – *Trade lines* means credit cards or other revolving accounts. Not having a credit card doesn't help your credit. Even if you never use it, you should have a credit card just to help your credit.

The numbers generated by each credit bureau are usually similar, but not always. Banks will typically report to their preferred credit bureau only, and then that bureau shares the information with the others. Depending on timing, information may not have disseminated across all bureaus.

No Credit

It is possible not to have a credit score at all. Most young people (*cough*

Ashla) don't have a credit score. You start out in life with no score and begin to build one only while applying for loans or payment plans (such as some cell phones) that will check your credit and report your history.

Information (both good and bad) on your credit report falls off over time as well—typically, after ten years. So, on the opposite end of the spectrum, a lot of elderly people don't have credit scores or begin to see declines in their credit scores. These people may have never had a missed payment in their life. They are now towards the end of their life though, and all the loans that have been paid off are no longer being reflected on their credit report. So they lose their score and sometimes struggle with obtaining financing in their twilight years.

Not having credit often limits what you can get for your first loans. This results in higher rates and fees. There are ways to get around it though.

By the time I turned eighteen, I already had a credit score of just over 700, and I'd never had a loan or needed to make payments on anything yet.

How?

My parents had the foresight to add me as an authorized signer on one of their credit cards, and they managed their credit very well. They did this when I was about fifteen, so I ended up with three years of good credit history. I was able to obtain my own credit cards at that point.

Some parents out there right now are panicking at the thought of giving their child a credit card and access to thousands of dollars of credit available. To those parents I have one suggestion to give: You need to work more on money management with your kids. However, the simple solution is that you don't actually give your kids the credit card. My parents held on to the card until I was sixteen, working, and driving. I used cash for most of my personal transactions and used the card for only those items that my parents approved (such as buying new tires for my car). I also had it in case of emergencies.

Being added to someone else's credit card as an authorized signer works only if the person with the credit card keeps their affairs in order. If they make a habit of maxing out their card or pay late a couple of times, it negatively affects both people.

Building Credit

Getting added as an authorized signer on someone else's credit card is a great way to start building credit, but it also carries the risk that the other person may not be good with their money. There are other ways for you to start building credit:

1. The one I have heard recommended most often is a secured credit card. This is when you send the credit card company $500, and they send you a credit card with a $500 limit. In the event you don't pay, they keep all or some of the $500, depending on what you owe, and close the card. This protects the credit card company and gives you the opportunity to learn cash management skills. In the event you are a good customer, you may be able to graduate to an unsecured line with the credit card company, they send you the $500 back, and you get to keep the card. Most of what I have heard is that you end up needing to close the old card and get a new card to get back your original $500.

2. Similar to a secured credit card are cash-secured credit builder loans. This was my favorite way to help people looking to build, or re-build, their credit. The most common way to structure this is to deposit money (typically, $1,000) into a savings account. You then use that money as collateral (security) for a loan of $1,000 at the same bank. So you get your $1,000 right back. You then make payments (preferably, automatic) to the bank for six to twenty-four months. I used to prefer at least twelve months to establish a longer history. This loan is pretty cheap to get with a minimal loan fee, and then the interest rate is usually one-three percent over the interest rate you are earning on the savings. I like it because it can be cheaper than other loan alternatives; it doesn't require any large amount of cash out of pocket for more than a few days that it takes to set up the loan (because you deposit the money and then get it leant right back to you); and because when the loan is paid off you get the money in the savings account released back to you, so it works as a forced savings. During the time you are making payments, the bank should be reporting to the credit bureau each month. Also, since it is a cash-secured loan, banks usually don't require a good credit score or even credit to be checked in order to set them up.

3. In the event you can't make a payment, you can ask the bank to use the savings account to pay off the loan. This helps prevent you from a payment default. Also, once the loan is paid off, you would receive any remaining funds in the savings account that weren't used to pay off the loan. These types of loans usually don't make the banks any money because they receive so little interest and fees from them so some banks won't bother with them unless you are using a much

higher dollar amount. I have heard that local and small regional banks[8] are more likely to do these types of loans than big banks are.

4. Student loans are a big contributor to building credit among young adults. I hate them. I think they are a trap that unfairly encourages young people who may not be college appropriate or may not need a college degree in their preferred field to go to school and spend money they don't have for something they don't need. However, federal student loans are easy to get, and payments don't need to be made until you are done with college for six months. Payments are deferred until that time. They are reported on your credit report the entire time you have them though. So it looks like you are maintaining good credit habits, even though you aren't really doing anything with the loans.

5. Another way that a lot of people start building credit is when they get their first car loan. To secure financing, auto lenders often require a co-signer or guarantor. A co-signer (a.k.a. co-borrower or co-maker) is someone with good credit that agrees to be on the loan with you. All the on-time payments (or late payments) get reported on both of your credit reports. The bank has the right to call your co-signer and discuss with them the details of the loan, including all payments. The co-signer is just as financially responsible for the loan as you are and will be on the hook to make payments if you don't.

6. A guarantor is used less frequently for personal loans, but you see them a lot with business loans. A guarantor is guaranteeing that the lender won't lose money. Lenders typically don't contact guarantors until a loan is being collected (via either repossession, judgment, or foreclosure). This protects the guarantor from all the late payments that the other person might have racked up. However, they could see a judgment end up on their credit if they don't make things right for the bank. With either a guarantor or a co-signer, someone without credit (or with bad credit) can get access to most of the same loans and credit cards that a person with good credit has access to.

Maintaining Credit

Once you start building credit, it is pretty simple to ensure that you maintain good credit. The basic premise is that you do everything that you agreed to do when you signed the loan paperwork. The one item you have the most

---

[8] Think "Bank of *Your Town*" versus Wells Fargo.

control over is ensuring you make your payments on time! Late payments have the quickest negative impact on your credit score. Here are three ways to maintain good credit and continue to improve your score:

1. Most loans and credit card companies are happy to help you make on time payments by setting you up with auto pay. Auto pay (a.k.a. automatic payments) allows the lender to reach into your bank account on a pre-determined day (e.g., the first of the month) for a set period (e.g., five years) and take out the agreed-upon payment. This helps them and it helps you. In this scenario, the only time you would be late, and have it be your fault, is if there was no money in the account for the lender to access.

2. In addition to making on-time payments, you will want to avoid events such as repossession and foreclosures (both of which can be avoided by making your payments on time each month). A repossession is fairly quick and allows the bank to show up and take the stuff that they lent you money on (most commonly, a vehicle). A foreclosure takes longer because it is typically tied to your home or other real estate you own (see Chapter 18 for more information in foreclosures).

3. Another negative event to avoid is a judgment. Judgments can come from a couple of places. The most likely one comes from not paying your agreed loan and there not being enough (if any) collateral (such as a car) for the lender to get their money out of from reselling it. They can pursue a judgment, which gets filed with the courts and requires you to pay back whatever amount you still owe. These can be attached to real estate (a home you own), and when you sell that in the future, the bank will get repaid from the proceeds of the sale. Other judgments can stem from injuring someone and their suing you. Or a big one is a tax judgment. This is when you don't pay your taxes, so the government files a judgment against you for non-payment.

Fixing Credit

In the event that you make a few mistakes (and most of us do), you should know that there are steps you can take to fix your credit. None of these steps are a magic wand to repair your credit instantly, but they can help you. Fixing credit and building credit are very similar, and some steps can overlap. Below are four steps to help you review your credit report:

1. First, you need to know what your credit is. Go to annualcreditreport.com to get a free credit report. You can get one every twelve months from each of the three credit bureaus. This report does not show your score but does show your current and a lot of your past accounts. You want to check and make sure all of the accounts are ones you recognize[9] as being yours. Then, check to see whether any of the accounts are reporting late payments or charged-off amounts. A *charge-off* is the amount the lender has determined they can't get back from you, so they strike it from their books and report it to the credit agencies. If you have accounts showing up that aren't yours or that list incorrectly reported payments and charge-offs, then you should start a dispute immediately. The website has buttons next to each account for you to do this.

2. Your report should also reflect any data about addresses you've lived at, your birth year, names you go by, phone numbers you've had, spouses, and employers. Review these as well, and file disputes on any items that are incorrect. I once had a customer that had a name shared by someone in the next town over. Her credit was good, but the other lady's was awful. She had to constantly dispute items on her credit because the credit bureaus thought they were the same person, since their towns were so close together.

3. Credit reports will also show any public records. Typically, these are judgments, evictions, foreclosures, bankruptcies, and any repossessions that had to go through the courts (see chapters 6, 13, and 18 for more information on these). I have never seen an item show up in the public records section that had a positive impact on credit. While these items may end up being true, you will want to be proactive and add comments, if allowed, so that anyone pulling your credit gets your side of the story, without having to confront you about it.

4. Lastly, you will want to review the Inquiries. These are divided up into Hard Inquiries and Soft Inquiries. A **Hard Inquiry** is made by a company looking to extend credit to you. A **Soft Inquiry** is usually automated checks made by your existing lenders to make sure you are still handling all of your commitments well. While it is not as easy to dispute inquiries, you want to check and make sure that they are

---

[9] Sometimes older/closed accounts will change names, as companies are bought out. Don't be alarmed by this as long as the information is positive.

being made by companies you expect. If random companies are checking your credit, it may indicate that your identity has been compromised (chapter 19) and you need to take steps to protect yourself.

Once you've gotten and reviewed your credit report, there are many steps you can take to start fixing your credit. Below is a list of seven things you can do to help improve your credit score:

1. Disputing any negative remarks on your credit is the best course of action to cleaning up your credit quickly. It works only if they are incorrect, though. Otherwise you won't be making much progress by doing so. Sometimes you can also reach out to companies that may be reporting charge-offs or collection accounts and offer to repay amounts owed if they remove items from your credit report. I have seen this done more successfully with some collection companies[10] than with banks.

2. While it takes time, the best way to make long-lasting positive changes to your credit is to make sure everything is paid on time. Set yourself up for automatic payments so you don't miss anything.

3. You also want to start paying down balances, especially on credit cards. Cards with a high balance-to-limit ratio negatively affect your credit, so you want to get those down first. Doing so quickly will also help your credit fairly fast.

4. Once you get your credit cards paid down to zero, DO NOT CLOSE THEM, as counterintuitive as it seems. An open card with a zero balance shows that you can handle credit and helps your ratios. A closed card doesn't have as much positive impact. Cut the cards up to keep you from using them, but don't shut down the account.

5. A counterintuitive item is to ask the credit card companies to raise your limits. This works well with small-limit cards, like those with only a $500 limit. If you put $450 on the card every month and pay it off with statement, then the credit card is constantly reporting a 90

---

[10] A collection company is a business that specializes in getting money from people on loans or accounts that they didn't pay. Banks may sell bad loans to a collection company at a discount, then any money the collection company gets from the borrower first goes to repay the amount the collection company paid for the loan, then pays the collection company for their effort. Often, the collection company will add extra fees, so long as they are legally allowed, in order to make more money.

percent balance on the card, which is a bad ratio to have. If the credit company is willing, they may raise your limit to $1,000 in which case you have only a 45 percent usage, which looks much better. Just be careful not to get carried away with your new limits and start charging more. The level of usage, or balance-to-limit ratio, is important to banks because a high level could mean that the person has no extra credit available in case of an emergency. It could also mean that the person likes to spend every dollar they get rather than pay down debt or save (both of which indicate a borrower that is unlikely to continue making payments if they do experience a financial hardship). Alternatively, a low balance-to-limit ratio means that a borrow is likely good at handling their money.

6.   Another way to improve your credit by taking on more debt is to take out a debt consolidation loan. These personal loans can be taken out to pay off credit card debt. Loans do not have the same ratio rules that impact your credit that credit cards have. So if you pay off all your cards with a loan and then DON'T CHARGE MORE, you can help improve your credit score.

7.   Other ways to improve credit are the same as what I talked about earlier in this chapter for building credit in the first place. They include getting a secured credit card, getting a credit builder loan, and becoming an authorized co-signer on someone else's cards that are in good standing.

Opting Out of Credit

There are some ways to get around utilizing credit, but they are expensive. Buy-here-pay-here car dealerships and furniture galleries are more likely to extend a loan to you when you have bad credit or no credit. If you are in a tough spot, I can see why financing a low-cost car this way to get you to work may be beneficial. However, these financing options are very expensive. Rarely do any of the options listed below report to the credit bureaus, meaning you won't get any help improving your credit score.

I once financed a couple of buy-here-pay-here car dealerships, and they expected to repossess at least 35 percent of the vehicles they sold. They had to charge high interest to make it worthwhile to deal with this. The interest rates at these companies were three to four times higher than at traditional bank financing.

One of the car dealers also told me that he purposely doesn't report to the credit bureaus, because then his customers would be able to get better financing elsewhere. So beware that some of these places can be very predatory and take advantage of people in bad situations.

Payday loans are another option to borrow money, but they are slowly being killed off by legislation. I worked as a payday lender in 2008 and 2009, when it was the only full-time job I could find. I hated it. I felt like the company was forcing me to take advantage of people that could least afford it. If someone who lived paycheck to paycheck and had no savings had an emergency when they needed money, they could come to the payday lender and write us a check that we wouldn't cash until their payday.

However, we would give them $500, and they would write us a check for $575. Those borrowing from these institutions were not the most educated, so they would look at this and think it was only costing them 15%. When in reality they would come in every pay period to re-borrow the money, because they had no way of paying it off, as they had already been living paycheck to paycheck.

If they were getting paid every two weeks, they were paying $75 each time. With twenty-six pay periods a year, they paid $1,950 in interest each year for borrowing $500, or 390 percent.

I did see a couple of people that would come in and then borrow less and less each time until they no longer needed to borrow. That was one of the best ways to work themselves out of those loans. Many states now require payday lenders to offer payment plans that limit interest and offer a way for people to repay their loans. I recommend avoiding these loans at all costs. Like buy-here-pay-here, they are unlikely to report your good payment activity to a credit bureau, because they want to keep their customers returning to them.

Your last option for avoiding credit is the simplest—pay cash for everything. This can be very difficult to do, but I did deal with a couple of people when I was in banking that had no credit score because they had always paid cash for everything. Their family had money, and when they needed a car or a home they borrowed it from the family and repaid the family. This eliminated their interest expense and kept money in the family. If you can pay cash, you should. Don't pay interest unless you have to.

Why I Want My Daughter to Know This

If money makes the world go around, then credit gives you the key to access money. Not many people start out in life with a lot of money, so having access to money is important to get ahead in life. Having good credit allows you to purchase homes and vehicles at lower interest rates. It allows you to avoid deposits when setting up utilities. Credit is also a key component in obtaining business and investment loans if that is the route you choose to take.

Building and maintaining good credit will save you thousands of dollars in interest over a lifetime. That money can be used to reduce debt, save towards big purchases, make investments, or just have fun with. Personally, I'd rather spend $5 on coffee or $5,000 on a vacation than give that money to a lender when I don't have to.

There are relatively few ways to get around using credit. Those ways can be used for short periods of time but are not long-term solutions. They can also be expensive, so you are better off learning to play by the rules of credit than trying to avoid it.

7: LOANS

"Dad, what's interest?"

"Interest is what you pay to the bank for the loan."

Blank stare.

"If you want to borrow someone else's money, they want you to pay them back and then pay them for lending you the money."

"Why would I do that?"

"Well, if you want to buy something right now, and you don't have the money, you would get a loan."

"But then I have to pay more money."

"Yes, but sometimes it makes more sense to buy something now and pay interest than to wait until you save up the money."

Another blank stare.

"For example, if you wanted to buy a new toy that cost $10 today, and you didn't have the money. You could wait until you have $10, or you could get a loan and pay the $10 plus maybe another dollar to the bank, making the total amount you paid $11. This makes sense if you think that toy is going to cost $15 tomorrow or if the toy is really worth $11 to you."

Ashla's brow furrowed as her young mind thought this over.

"Dad, can I have $10?"

The best time to apply for a loan is when you don't need the money. This seems like the dumbest thing in the world, but it is absolutely true. As both a lender and a prolific borrower, I can tell you that it is way easier to get a loan when you don't need it.

When you need a loan, it typically means you are strapped for cash. You may have a medical emergency or an unexpected car repair. You may have been out of work due to injury or sickness and just need a little money to get by.

When you *need* money, you can't get your hands on it fast enough. Your stress level is going to be high because you can't see past your current predicament. Bankers have an innate sense when someone is desperate, and it is an immediate red flag. Bankers want to know how you got into the situation you are in. Why the money will help you. How you will repay the money. And what you will do to avoid getting into this situation again in the future.

Think you can avoid this by using an online lending platform? Think again. Having a human in charge of a lending decision helps because they can be empathetic. They can provide coaching as to alternatives or what you could do in the future to do better.

Because online platforms cut out the human element, they can't see a loan request for the person that is behind it. Online lenders are more likely to have higher credit standards, making it more difficult for people to get loans. These are built into their algorithms as a way to avoid unnecessary risk.

With a little advanced planning, you can avoid the heartache of being in *need* of money. I'm not talking about saving and keeping a reserve of money to access. While that is probably the best way, it is often out of reach of many people. At one point, I was pretty happy with about $3,000 in savings until my sewer pipe broke, and the repairs that weren't covered by insurance[11] added up to $6,000. That wiped out my savings and left me in need of more money.

At the time this happened, I had close to $12k in credit card debt with less than $3,000 to go before I was maxed out. My credit scores were already hurting from the high ratio of balances to limits. This was a point in my life when I *needed* money. It was a struggle, and we had some family help to get through it. I made a commitment to myself to never be back in that position.[12]

So we saved again, but we also realized we needed access to money in case something bad happened before we got our savings rebuilt. When we were able to, we opened a second credit card that we rarely used. This

---

[11] The repairs were not covered by insurance because a sewer pipe is not considered part of your home. Homeowners' insurance cover from the walls in. The pipe break was in the ground twenty feet from the home.

[12] We were living close to hand-to-mouth at the time—saving maybe $50 a month. This situation forced us to evaluate our budget again and see what other cuts we could make. We were already super conservative in our spending, but we managed to cut almost $300 in monthly expenses. See last chapter 21 for what we did.

instantly gave us access to $5,000 more in the event of a disaster. Following that, we opened up a Home Equity Line of Credit (HELOC). A HELOC functions similarly to a credit card, but it is secured against the equity[13] in your home.

Since then, we have kept available balances on our credit cards and money available on our HELOC. At various points, we've also had some small business lines of credit to help with fluctuations (up and down changes) in cash flow and larger expenses such as new furnaces. It has made our life much easier to manage.

Having credit cards in your name that you aren't using gives you access to that money when you need it. Owning a home, you can use a HELOC for the same purpose. By planning ahead you give yourself more options and more time, and reduce the stress that comes along with being in *need* of money.

Similar examples include getting a vehicle or home loan when you don't need it. Getting a loan to buy a home is a stressful process because the bank wants all sorts of weird documentation and you are on a timeline to get it to them or you can't buy the house. When you go to refinance a house,[14] you aren't working against the clock. It is a much more relaxed process.

Common Lending Terms

Before going any further, I think it is helpful to explain some basic lending terms so that everyone understands them. As a lender, I always tried to explain the basics of a loan to any new borrower that I dealt with. Over the six years I spent as a lender, I had only one borrower who actually read through all the loan documentation. That was on a multimillion-dollar loan, and the gentleman was a very astute businessman. This fact, I guess, proves that average borrowers don't read their paperwork, and the rich do.

To be fair, most lenders don't read their own documentation. I certainly didn't have time to read through every loan document from start to finish. However, we used standardized forms. So, I did read through everything

---

[13] Equity is the difference between what your home is worth and how much you owe on it. If you own a $250,000 home and owe $175,000 on the mortgage, you have $75,000 in equity.

[14] Refinancing is the process of replacing your existing loan with a new one. It is done for a variety of reasons, including to get a better rate, remove private mortgage insurance, change the length of the term, or remove one of the previous borrowers.

once. Then, I got used to looking for the items that could change, and I would just look for them.

Here are the common terms you will see when looking through loan documents:

- Term – The length of the loan.[15] Sometimes this is quoted in years of months.

- Interest Rate – Expressed as a percentage (%), this number is multiplied by your outstanding balance then divided by twelve to determine your monthly payment.[16]

- Origination (Loan) Fee – This is a dollar amount that is charged up front as part of the cost of getting the loan. This amount is typically rolled into the loan balance and becomes part of the principal that you need to pay back to the bank over time.

- APR (Annual Percentage Rate) – This number converts any origination fees into a percentage rate and adds it to the interest rate. Confused yet? Banks are required by law to show you information in this manner. Here is the formula:
    - APR = (((Fees$ + Interest$) / number of days of loan) x 365) x 100)
    - Still confused? Don't worry about it. The key to APR is that it's purpose is to allow you to compare products easily with different fee and interest rate structures. If you are looking across ten loans with ten different origination fees and ten different interest rates, you may get confused by that too. Compare the APRs of all of them, which are required by law to be part of consumer (personal) loans. The one with the lowest APR costs you the least amount of money.

- Collateral (Security) – This is something tangible that you pledge for the loan. In the event you default on the loan, the bank can come get this and sell it to get their money back. The most common types of collateral are vehicles and real estate, but don't let this limit your imagination. I've seen art, coins, other people's cash, intellectual property (such as patents or books), and stock—all used as collateral for personal loans.

---

[15] Loans are also referred to as notes or promissory notes (because you are "promising" to repay it).
[16] This is for a rough estimate only.

- Default – This is the term used to describe when you stop abiding by the conditions of the loan agreement. The most common type of default is when you stop making payments. There are hundreds of other types of default. Another common one is failing to keep the collateral insured properly. The bank spells out in the loan paperwork all the types of default that they can consider as a breach of contract. This leads to next steps such as repossession (see chapter 18 for more about repossession).

- Personal Guarantee – This is your promise to repay the loan no matter what. If it is a business loan, the personal guarantee is there to assure the bank that if the business fails, you will personally pay back the loan. This allows the bank to pursue other assets (such as a home or stocks) that you own outside of the business and that are not used as collateral for the loan.

Common Types of Loans

- Vehicle Loans – typically, two to seven years in length, secured by a vehicle for the purpose of purchasing a car or refinancing an existing vehicle loan.

- Personal (Signature) Loans – usually one to five years in length, used to refinance other debt, with many used to consolidate credit card debt. These are unsecured.

- Home Loans (First Mortgage) – fifteen to thirty years in length, used to purchase or refinance a home and secured by your home.

- Second Mortgages and Home Equity Loans – typically ten to twenty years in length, these can be used with a first mortgage to help purchase a more expensive home. They also can be used to consolidate larger amounts of debt or take money out of your home for a large purchase.

- Home Equity Line of Credit – like a second mortgage, secured against your home after the first mortgage. It operates like a credit card when you can take money out and pay it back only to take it back out again. They can be from five to ten years in length and then can have either an automatic term of five to ten years (meaning any balance is divided into regular payments for you to pay it off) or the entire balance due (which requires you to either refinance it into another HELOC, Home Equity Loan, or simply pay it off).

- Credit cards – These are fairly easy to get and are unsecured (unless you specifically set it up secured against something). They have high interest rates and allow you to easily spend money just about everywhere. Be careful with these, as you can rack up a lot of debt on them very quickly. The minimum monthly payment is so low and has so little going towards repaying principal (most goes towards interest) that it can take a long time to pay them off. Check your balances regularly throughout the month so you understand what you are spending. To avoid getting into trouble, you should pay your credit card off every month. You can earn free stuff like travel or gift cards by using a credit card. But it doesn't make sense if you suddenly have to start paying them high amounts of interest.

Putting Your Best Foot Forward

Want to ensure your greatest probability of successfully obtaining a loan? There are a number of things you can do to increase your odds of success.

1. Know your own numbers. You should know how much money you are spending currently on debt payments. You should also know how much money you are making each month, both gross and net.[17] Knowing your numbers makes it much easier for lenders to calculate whether they can help you or not up front.

2. Be prepared. Fill out the application as completely as possible. At the time you hand in the application, come prepared with any required documentation. For small loans, this may just be your most recent paystub.[18] For mortgages, you may need a lot more documentation.

3. Be easy to work with and quick to provide extra information. Be available to answer the phone and emails quickly. If the lender is requesting more documentation, get it to them as fast as you can and don't take more than twenty-four hours. This keeps your loan request moving forward and makes the lender like you.

4. Be honest. Don't try to hide anything. Sometimes lenders don't need your information, so you can verbally discuss items with them and let

---

[17] Gross income is how much money you make before taxes, retirement contributions, and other withholdings are taken out of your check. Net income is how much money you have left and gets deposited into your account.

[18] A paystub is issued by your employer every time you get paid. It shows how much you've earned, what was withheld to pay income taxes (next chapter 8), and what your net pay is.

the lender decide whether they need to see documentation. When applying for personal mortgages, I always talk to the lender about my business loans. Most of the time, they don't want to see them because then they have to see all the supporting tax returns and bank statements for the businesses as well. If they can't qualify me for the loan without that information, they let me know.

5. Be willing to learn from the lender. Lenders know a lot more about loans than you do. Even though I was a lender, I assume that the lender I am talking to knows more about making loans at *their* bank than I do. I try to listen and ask questions so I can understand what the lender is doing and why.

6. Learn from your mistakes—which brings us to the next section.

Denial

Bankers are people, and like most people they hate delivering bad news. I never delivered bad news on Fridays because I didn't want to ruin my client's weekend. Delivering bad news on a Friday means that the person can't talk to other lenders until Monday, so they just have to sit and think about it all weekend. For the same reason, I tried never to deliver bad news after 3:00 p.m. I felt that people didn't need to take that home with them. This way, they could also have a couple hours to talk to other banks and get a new solution started. I also tried not to deliver bad news before 9 a.m. I didn't want to risk catching someone at a bad time of day when they, being one of many grouchy morning people, weren't thinking clearly yet.

That being said, the people that I saw be the most successful following a rejection were the ones that took the news with the most grace. They didn't raise their voice or get defensive. They listened and asked questions. Because they weren't yelling at me, I was happy to answer any questions as a way to provide some sort of value or comfort to them, following the bad news. Once I realized these people were learning from their denials and moving forward, I began to do the same thing.

What I learned from this is that the calmer you are when facing rejection the more likely someone will want to help you in other ways. They may offer advice to improve your loan application or guide you to another bank that may be a better fit for you.

I have listed my four best questions below to ask a lender when you've been turned down for a personal or business loan:

1. What recommendations do you have? (Nice open-ended question)
2. What can I do to change the request so it could get approved? (Get a co-signer, put more money down, choose a less expensive vehicle/home, etc.)
3. What banks or lenders do you know that may be willing to make me this loan? (Banks have different standards and risk tolerances.)
4. What are the key reasons for why I am being declined? (Identify the problems so you can come up with solutions.)

In my career as a banker, I denied more loans than I approved not because of the person or because I was in a bad mood that day. I didn't enjoy denying loans. Generally, denying a loan means crushing someone's hope or dream. It can be a hope to drive a new car or a dream to start their own business.

Generally, loan denials for both personal and business loans fall into the following categories:

-   The borrower isn't ready: Perhaps the borrower doesn't have enough of a down payment, needs to improve their credit score or doesn't have enough income to pay back the loan.
-   The idea isn't ready: For a personal loan, this can mean that they want to buy a car but are looking at vehicles that are too expensive for their budget. For a business, this can be that they haven't spent enough time putting together a business plan and going through their financial information to see whether it will work.
-   The bank isn't ready: Banks are not created equal. Some banks like home mortgages. Other banks like agricultural business loans. Others like airplane loans. Rarely do you find a bank that likes all types of loans *and* is good at making all those types of loans. Different banks like different loans. Your loan may not fit this bank but may be a perfect fit at another bank. Keep looking.

As a lender, I loved helping people achieve success by using a loan. I loved learning about peoples' businesses or listening to them talk about how great their new home was going to be. I also enjoyed being able to counsel people and help them make intelligent business or financial decisions.

Why I Want My Daughter to Know This

Having a basic knowledge of how loans work takes the fear out of borrowing money and allows you to communicate more intelligently and effectively with lenders. I think fear of being denied and looking stupid hold people back more than anything else. If you can learn enough to abate the fear, then you can achieve great things.

I also want my daughter to continue to grow throughout life. I think if she is faced with denials here and there but has the tools to learn from them that she will naturally grow. Each obstacle will become a new learning experience, and nothing will truly be able to hold her back.

8: TAXES

"Dad, kids under eighteen shouldn't have to pay sales tax."

"Oh yeah? Why is that?" I asked.

"It's taxation without representation! The government is allowed to tax our income for four years before we are given the right to vote at eighteen. It's like we fought a revolution over this or something!"

"Unfortunately, you can't buy a gun until you are eighteen either, so you aren't likely to overthrow the government anytime soon…"

"That's stupid. We shouldn't have to pay taxes!"

"Or you should be given the right to vote."

"Yeah, people that are fourteen should be allowed to vote! We are productive members of society and paying taxes."

"But how do you adjust for kids who don't work until they turn sixteen or until they get out of high school?" I pointed out, thinking she would be stumped by this.

"Not all adults work either," she countered. "They still get to vote."

I was stumped.

After college, I worked for a couple of seasons with Liberty Tax Service. In order to work with Liberty Tax, I had to attend their in-person class for several weeks and then pass a test. I'd already been preparing my own taxes for years and had learned how to prepare my taxes by hand when I was in high school, so the class was pretty easy for me. I did, however, really enjoy going through tax returns form by form and calculating credits, income, and exemptions by hand. The experience gave me a deeper understanding of how everything fit together.

Unfortunately, we have become more and more removed from preparing our own taxes. Quick service tax companies such as Liberty Tax, H&R Block, and Jackson Hewitt put the burden onto someone else and take a lot of the pain out of the process. These companies target the people that don't understand or don't want to understand how to do taxes. Most of their business comes from low-income filers. When I worked at Liberty Tax, we did about 80 percent of our business for the year in the first thirty days of tax season (roughly, January 15–February 15) as we helped the rush of people that were desperate to get their tax refunds. Due to their target clientele, the training focused on the basic needs of these people who had very simple tax returns. The cost of these services was similar to having an accountant prepare taxes (think hundreds of dollars), but the benefit to the people using them was that most of the time that money could be taken out of the tax refund they were getting, so they didn't have to come up with the money to pay.

If you have a bit of patience and are willing to learn something new, programs like TurboTax allow you to do the work yourself and save a lot of the cost of getting your taxes prepared. TurboTax even has a small business version that allows you to prepare your own taxes for LLCs and corporations.

However, the more successful you get in life the more likely you are to have a variety of investments, possibly own your own business or two, and have complex income structures from several different sources. When you get to this point, googling for answers to your tax questions just won't cut it anymore, and you need to seek the advice of a tax professional.[19]

Before you read any further, please note that I am not a tax or legal professional. Anything that follows is not advice but is information only. I do not guarantee the accuracy of the information. Everyone's situation is unique. If you have questions about your situation, you should seek advice from your own accountants, bookkeepers, lawyers, or other advisors.

Income

When people talk about taxes, they usually talk about income taxes. This chapter focuses just on income taxes, but there are property taxes (taxes paid each year on a home you own). Income taxes are taxes you pay on income you earn. The income tax system is designed so that, in general, the more you

---

[19] Notice that I haven't mentioned a CPA (Certified Public Accountant). I used a CPA for a while and had a bad experience. At the time of this writing, I use a Certified Bookkeeper & Enrolled Agent, which means she is not an accountant. I have gotten much better advice and established a better relationship with her than I ever did with the accountant I used previously.

make the more you pay.

Most people start off with a part-time job in high school or college to earn some spending money. Normally, this path eventually turns into a full-time job once out of school. This type of income is considered earned income, and employers take care of withholdings[20] for federal and state taxes as well as Social Security and Medicare withholdings. You have to fill out Form W-4, Employee's Withholding Certificate, which determines how much money will be withheld from your income to pay for taxes. If you are a young single person with no kids and earning a lot of money, you will have more withheld than a modest income earner with a family (see more on this later in this chapter under deductions & credits). How you fill out your W-4 has a direct impact on your net pay, and you can see the results on your paystub.[21]

---

[20] Withholdings is money taken out of your paycheck at the time you earn it and sent to the government on your behalf for taxes.

[21] The second page of Form W-4 is instructions (not pictured) and walks you through how you should be filling out the form. If you have questions about it ask your company's HR (Human Resources) person.

W-4 Example

Form **W-4**	**Employee's Withholding Certificate**	OMB No. 1545-0074
Department of the Treasury Internal Revenue Service	▶ Complete Form W-4 so that your employer can withhold the correct federal income tax from your pay. ▶ Give Form W-4 to your employer. ▶ Your withholding is subject to review by the IRS.	20**20**

Step 1:
Enter Personal Information

(a) First name and middle initial	Last name	(b) Social security number

Address

City or town, state, and ZIP code

▶ Does your name match the name on your social security card? If not, to ensure you get credit for your earnings, contact SSA at 800-772-1213 or go to www.ssa.gov.

(c) ☐ Single or Married filing separately
☐ Married filing jointly (or Qualifying widow(er))
☐ Head of household (Check only if you're unmarried and pay more than half the costs of keeping up a home for yourself and a qualifying individual.)

Complete Steps 2–4 ONLY if they apply to you; otherwise, skip to Step 5. See page 2 for more information on each step, who can claim exemption from withholding, when to use the online estimator, and privacy.

Step 2:
Multiple Jobs or Spouse Works

Complete this step if you (1) hold more than one job at a time, or (2) are married filing jointly and your spouse also works. The correct amount of withholding depends on income earned from all of these jobs.

Do **only one** of the following.

(a) Use the estimator at *www.irs.gov/W4App* for most accurate withholding for this step (and Steps 3–4); **or**

(b) Use the Multiple Jobs Worksheet on page 3 and enter the result in Step 4(c) below for roughly accurate withholding; **or**

(c) If there are only two jobs total, you may check this box. Do the same on Form W-4 for the other job. This option is accurate for jobs with similar pay; otherwise, more tax than necessary may be withheld . . . . . ▶ ☐

TIP: To be accurate, submit a 2020 Form W-4 for all other jobs. If you (or your spouse) have self-employment income, including as an independent contractor, use the estimator.

Complete Steps 3–4(b) on Form W-4 for only ONE of these jobs. Leave those steps blank for the other jobs. (Your withholding will be most accurate if you complete Steps 3–4(b) on the Form W-4 for the highest paying job.)

Step 3:
Claim Dependents

If your income will be $200,000 or less ($400,000 or less if married filing jointly):

Multiply the number of qualifying children under age 17 by $2,000 ▶ $ _____

Multiply the number of other dependents by $500 . . . . ▶ $ _____

Add the amounts above and enter the total here . . . . | **3** | $ |

Step 4 (optional):
Other Adjustments

(a) **Other income (not from jobs).** If you want tax withheld for other income you expect this year that won't have withholding, enter the amount of other income here. This may include interest, dividends, and retirement income . . . . | **4(a)** | $ |

(b) **Deductions.** If you expect to claim deductions other than the standard deduction and want to reduce your withholding, use the Deductions Worksheet on page 3 and enter the result here . . . . | **4(b)** | $ |

(c) **Extra withholding.** Enter any additional tax you want withheld each **pay period** . | **4(c)** | $ |

Step 5:
Sign Here

Under penalties of perjury, I declare that this certificate, to the best of my knowledge and belief, is true, correct, and complete.

▶ _____
Employee's signature (This form is not valid unless you sign it.)

▶ _____
Date

Employers Only	Employer's name and address	First date of employment	Employer identification number (EIN)

For Privacy Act and Paperwork Reduction Act Notice, see page 3.   Cat. No. 10220Q   Form **W-4** (2020)

At the end of the year, your employer will then give you Form W-2, Wage and Tax Statement, which will list exactly how much your gross income was for the year and how much you had withheld for taxes, Social Security, and Medicare. If you had any other withholdings for items like retirement accounts, the form will also have that information on it. You will use this information to prepare your income tax return for the year.

W-2 Example

22222	a Employee's social security number	OMB No. 1545-0008		
b Employer identification number (EIN)		1 Wages, tips, other compensation	2 Federal income tax withheld	
c Employer's name, address, and ZIP code		3 Social security wages	4 Social security tax withheld	
		5 Medicare wages and tips	6 Medicare tax withheld	
		7 Social security tips	8 Allocated tips	
d Control number		9	10 Dependent care benefits	
e Employee's first name and initial Last name Suff.		11 Nonqualified plans	12a	
		13 Statutory employee Retirement plan Third-party sick pay	12b	
		14 Other	12c	
			12d	
f Employee's address and ZIP code				
15 State Employer's state ID number	16 State wages, tips, etc.	17 State income tax	18 Local wages, tips, etc.	19 Local income tax	20 Locality name

W-2 Wage and Tax Statement   **2019**   Department of the Treasury—Internal Revenue Service
Form
Copy 1—For State, City, or Local Tax Department

Once you start earning money, you will start having to complete a tax return every year. The basic tax return that people fill out is called Form 1040, U.S. Individual Income Tax Return. On the next two pages is an example of Form 1040. If you have a simple situation, this two-page form may be the only one you need. As you do more things with your life and money, you will have more forms to fill out. Those forms follow later. As you are starting out, your focus should be just on this form.

Form 1040 is designed to be self-explanatory and asks you questions you need to answer directly on the form. For your first year, you should need only your name, address, social security number, and your Form W-2 from your employer. Form 1040 does have instructions (not included), and you can find more answers on the IRS website. Entire books have been written to help people understand how to fill out tax returns. This chapter is designed to help make you familiar with it.

1040 Page 1 Example

1040 Page 2 Example

Form 1040 (2019)   Page **2**

12a	**Tax** (see inst.) Check if any from Form(s): **1** ☐ 8814 **2** ☐ 4972 **3** ☐ _____	12a		
b	Add Schedule 2, line 3, and line 12a and enter the total ▶		12b	
13a	Child tax credit or credit for other dependents	13a		
b	Add Schedule 3, line 7, and line 13a and enter the total ▶		13b	
14	Subtract line 13b from line 12b. If zero or less, enter -0-		14	
15	Other taxes, including self-employment tax, from Schedule 2, line 10		15	
16	Add lines 14 and 15. This is your **total tax** ▶		16	
17	Federal income tax withheld from Forms W-2 and 1099		17	
18	Other payments and refundable credits:			
a	Earned income credit (EIC)	18a		
b	Additional child tax credit. Attach Schedule 8812	18b		
c	American opportunity credit from Form 8863, line 8	18c		
d	Schedule 3, line 14	18d		
e	Add lines 18a through 18d. These are your **total other payments and refundable credits** ▶		18e	
19	Add lines 17 and 18e. These are your **total payments** ▶		19	
20	If line 19 is more than line 16, subtract line 16 from line 19. This is the amount you **overpaid**		20	
21a	Amount of line 20 you want **refunded to you.** If Form 8888 is attached, check here ☐ ▶		21a	
▶ b	Routing number _____	▶ c Type: ☐ Checking ☐ Savings		
▶ d	Account number _____			
22	Amount of line 20 you want **applied to your 2020 estimated tax** ▶	22		
23	**Amount you owe.** Subtract line 19 from line 16. For details on how to pay, see instructions ▶		23	
24	Estimated tax penalty (see instructions) ▶	24		

• If you have a qualifying child, attach Sch. EIC.
• If you have nontaxable combat pay, see instructions.

Refund
Direct deposit? See instructions.

Amount You Owe

Third Party Designee
(Other than paid preparer)

Do you want to allow another person (other than your paid preparer) to discuss this return with the IRS? See instructions. ☐ **Yes.** Complete below. ☐ **No**

Designee's name ▶ _____   Phone no. ▶ _____   Personal identification number (PIN) ▶ ☐☐☐☐☐

Sign Here
Joint return? See instructions. Keep a copy for your records.

Under penalties of perjury, I declare that I have examined this return and accompanying schedules and statements, and to the best of my knowledge and belief, they are true, correct, and complete. Declaration of preparer (other than taxpayer) is based on all information of which preparer has any knowledge.

Your signature	Date	Your occupation	If the IRS sent you an Identity Protection PIN, enter it here (see inst.) ☐☐☐☐☐☐
Spouse's signature. If a joint return, **both** must sign.	Date	Spouse's occupation	If the IRS sent your spouse an Identity Protection PIN, enter it here (see inst.) ☐☐☐☐☐☐

Phone no. _____   Email address _____

Paid Preparer Use Only

Preparer's name	Preparer's signature		Date	PTIN	Check if: ☐ 3rd Party Designee ☐ Self-employed
Firm's name ▶				Phone no.	
Firm's address ▶				Firm's EIN ▶	

Go to *www.irs.gov/Form1040* for instructions and the latest information.   Form **1040** (2019)

If you are considered a contract worker or a freelancer, you will have to fill out Form W-9 instead. Contract workers and freelancers are *NOT EMPLOYEES* of the company they are working for. This may be because it is part-time and/or temporary work. When you are considered a contractor, you are in business for yourself and are considered self-employed. You could perform the same work for another company. Some common types of contractors/freelancers include graphic designers, people working in trades such as roofers/plumbers/handymen, or personal trainers. However, these people could all be employees just as easily. It depends on whom they work for.

Form W-9 allows for the company you are contracted with to report the money they are paying you to the IRS and nothing else. *It is up to you to make all necessary payments to the government for taxes,*[22] and there are penalties if you don't. This sometimes makes it feel like you are making more money, because you are bringing home more out of each paycheck. However, when you work for another company you end up paying about 7.5 percent for Social Security and Medicare, and your employer pays a similar amount. When you are considered self-employed, you pay the full amount all by yourself.

---

[22] You will have to pay income taxes as normal and will also have self-employment tax of 15.3 percent, which replaces Social Security and Medicare.

W-9 Example

| Form **W-9**
 (Rev. October 2018)
 Department of the Treasury
 Internal Revenue Service | **Request for Taxpayer**
 Identification Number and Certification

 ▶ Go to *www.irs.gov/FormW9* for instructions and the latest information. | Give Form to the requester. Do not send to the IRS. |

1 Name (as shown on your income tax return). Name is required on this line; do not leave this line blank.

2 Business name/disregarded entity name, if different from above

3 Check appropriate box for federal tax classification of the person whose name is entered on line 1. Check only **one** of the following seven boxes.

☐ Individual/sole proprietor or single-member LLC   ☐ C Corporation   ☐ S Corporation   ☐ Partnership   ☐ Trust/estate

☐ Limited liability company. Enter the tax classification (C=C corporation, S=S corporation, P=Partnership) ▶ _____

Note: Check the appropriate box in the line above for the tax classification of the single-member owner. Do not check LLC if the LLC is classified as a single-member LLC that is disregarded from the owner unless the owner of the LLC is another LLC that is not disregarded from the owner for U.S. federal tax purposes. Otherwise, a single-member LLC that is disregarded from the owner should check the appropriate box for the tax classification of its owner.

☐ Other (see instructions) ▶

4 Exemptions (codes apply only to certain entities, not individuals; see instructions on page 3):

Exempt payee code (if any) _____

Exemption from FATCA reporting code (if any) _____

(Applies to accounts maintained outside the U.S.)

5 Address (number, street, and apt. or suite no.) See instructions.

Requester's name and address (optional)

6 City, state, and ZIP code

7 List account number(s) here (optional)

Print or type. See Specific Instructions on page 3.

Part I   Taxpayer Identification Number (TIN)

Enter your TIN in the appropriate box. The TIN provided must match the name given on line 1 to avoid backup withholding. For individuals, this is generally your social security number (SSN). However, for a resident alien, sole proprietor, or disregarded entity, see the instructions for Part I, later. For other entities, it is your employer identification number (EIN). If you do not have a number, see *How to get a TIN*, later.

Note: If the account is in more than one name, see the instructions for line 1. Also see *What Name and Number To Give the Requester* for guidelines on whose number to enter.

Social security number

☐☐☐ – ☐☐ – ☐☐☐☐

or

Employer identification number

☐☐ – ☐☐☐☐☐☐☐

Part II   Certification

Under penalties of perjury, I certify that:

1. The number shown on this form is my correct taxpayer identification number (or I am waiting for a number to be issued to me); and
2. I am not subject to backup withholding because: (a) I am exempt from backup withholding, or (b) I have not been notified by the Internal Revenue Service (IRS) that I am subject to backup withholding as a result of a failure to report all interest or dividends, or (c) the IRS has notified me that I am no longer subject to backup withholding; and
3. I am a U.S. citizen or other U.S. person (defined below); and
4. The FATCA code(s) entered on this form (if any) indicating that I am exempt from FATCA reporting is correct.

Certification instructions. You must cross out item 2 above if you have been notified by the IRS that you are currently subject to backup withholding because you have failed to report all interest and dividends on your tax return. For real estate transactions, item 2 does not apply. For mortgage interest paid, acquisition or abandonment of secured property, cancellation of debt, contributions to an individual retirement arrangement (IRA), and generally, payments other than interest and dividends, you are not required to sign the certification, but you must provide your correct TIN. See the instructions for Part II, later.

Sign Here | Signature of U.S. person ▶ | Date ▶

General Instructions

Section references are to the Internal Revenue Code unless otherwise noted.

Future developments. For the latest information about developments related to Form W-9 and its instructions, such as legislation enacted after they were published, go to *www.irs.gov/FormW9*.

Purpose of Form

An individual or entity (Form W-9 requester) who is required to file an information return with the IRS must obtain your correct taxpayer identification number (TIN) which may be your social security number (SSN), individual taxpayer identification number (ITIN), adoption taxpayer identification number (ATIN), or employer identification number (EIN), to report on an information return the amount paid to you, or other amount reportable on an information return. Examples of information returns include, but are not limited to, the following.

• Form 1099-INT (interest earned or paid)

• Form 1099-DIV (dividends, including those from stocks or mutual funds)

• Form 1099-MISC (various types of income, prizes, awards, or gross proceeds)

• Form 1099-B (stock or mutual fund sales and certain other transactions by brokers)

• Form 1099-S (proceeds from real estate transactions)

• Form 1099-K (merchant card and third party network transactions)

• Form 1098 (home mortgage interest), 1098-E (student loan interest), 1098-T (tuition)

• Form 1099-C (canceled debt)

• Form 1099-A (acquisition or abandonment of secured property)

Use Form W-9 only if you are a U.S. person (including a resident alien), to provide your correct TIN.

If you do not return Form W-9 to the requester with a TIN, you might be subject to backup withholding. See What is backup withholding, later.

Cat. No. 10231X   Form **W-9** (Rev. 10-2018)

As a contractor/freelancer, you will receive Form 1099-MISC Miscellaneous Income at the end of the year, which is what the company is reporting to the IRS for what they paid you. You will then complete Schedule C, Profit or Loss from Business as part of your tax return. The nice thing about being self-employed or considered a contract worker is that you are able to offset the income with expenses related to your job. For a time, my wife and I were both Zumba instructors. We were able to offset our income with things like the cost of our training and some travel expenses that were part of the business.

1099-Misc Example

Schedule C is also used if you decide to start a small business. If you are doing very well as a freelancer, you may decide to work for multiple companies and even have a few employees or subcontractors of your own. All of this would still be reported on Schedule C. Schedule C can even be used if you form a Limited Liability Company[23] (LLC) with just yourself, or yourself and your spouse as the only members. If you have other partners or other legal business entities, you will need to file different tax return forms.

---

[23] A Limited Liability Company or LLC is a simple company people can form to keep their business money and activities separate from the personal. This gives a level of professionalism as well as helps protect the person's personal money, home, and other assets in the event the business gets sued.

Schedule C Example

SCHEDULE C (Form 1040 or 1040-SR)		**Profit or Loss From Business** (Sole Proprietorship)		OMB No. 1545-0074
Department of the Treasury Internal Revenue Service (99)		▶ Go to www.irs.gov/ScheduleC for instructions and the latest information. ▶ Attach to Form 1040, 1040-SR, 1040-NR, or 1041; partnerships generally must file Form 1065.		20**19** Attachment Sequence No. 09

	Name of proprietor		Social security number (SSN)
A	Principal business or profession, including product or service (see instructions)		B Enter code from instructions ▶
C	Business name. If no separate business name, leave blank.		D Employer ID number (EIN) (see instr.)
E	Business address (including suite or room no.) ▶		
	City, town or post office, state, and ZIP code		
F	Accounting method: (1) ☐ Cash (2) ☐ Accrual (3) ☐ Other (specify) ▶		
G	Did you "materially participate" in the operation of this business during 2019? If "No," see instructions for limit on losses		☐ Yes ☐ No
H	If you started or acquired this business during 2019, check here . . . . ▶ ☐		
I	Did you make any payments in 2019 that would require you to file Form(s) 1099? (see instructions)		☐ Yes ☐ No
J	If "Yes," did you or will you file required Forms 1099?		☐ Yes ☐ No

Part I Income

1	Gross receipts or sales. See instructions for line 1 and check the box if this income was reported to you on Form W-2 and the "Statutory employee" box on that form was checked . . . . ▶ ☐	1
2	Returns and allowances	2
3	Subtract line 2 from line 1	3
4	Cost of goods sold (from line 42)	4
5	Gross profit. Subtract line 4 from line 3	5
6	Other income, including federal and state gasoline or fuel tax credit or refund (see instructions)	6
7	Gross income. Add lines 5 and 6 . . . . ▶	7

Part II Expenses. Enter expenses for business use of your home **only** on line 30.

8	Advertising . . .	8		18	Office expense (see instructions)	18
9	Car and truck expenses (see instructions) . . .	9		19	Pension and profit-sharing plans .	19
10	Commissions and fees .	10		20	Rent or lease (see instructions):	
11	Contract labor (see instructions)	11		a	Vehicles, machinery, and equipment	20a
12	Depletion . . .	12		b	Other business property . . .	20b
13	Depreciation and section 179 expense deduction (not included in Part III) (see instructions) . . .	13		21	Repairs and maintenance . . .	21
				22	Supplies (not included in Part III)	22
				23	Taxes and licenses	23
14	Employee benefit programs (other than on line 19) .	14		24	Travel and meals:	
15	Insurance (other than health)	15		a	Travel	24a
16	Interest (see instructions):			b	Deductible meals (see instructions)	24b
a	Mortgage (paid to banks, etc.)	16a		25	Utilities	25
b	Other . . .	16b		26	Wages (less employment credits)	26
17	Legal and professional services	17		27a	Other expenses (from line 48) . .	27a
				b	**Reserved for future use** . . .	27b
28	Total expenses before expenses for business use of home. Add lines 8 through 27a . . . . . ▶					28
29	Tentative profit or (loss). Subtract line 28 from line 7					29
30	Expenses for business use of your home. Do not report these expenses elsewhere. Attach Form 8829 unless using the simplified method (see instructions). **Simplified method filers only:** enter the total square footage of: (a) your home:_____ and (b) the part of your home used for business:_____ . Use the Simplified Method Worksheet in the instructions to figure the amount to enter on line 30					30
31	Net profit or (loss). Subtract line 30 from line 29. • If a profit, enter on both **Schedule 1 (Form 1040 or 1040-SR), line 3** (or **Form 1040-NR, line 13**) and on **Schedule SE, line 2**. (If you checked the box on line 1, see instructions). Estates and trusts, enter on **Form 1041, line 3.** • If a loss, you **must** go to line 32.					31
32	If you have a loss, check the box that describes your investment in this activity (see instructions). • If you checked 32a, enter the loss on both **Schedule 1 (Form 1040 or 1040-SR), line 3** (or **Form 1040-NR, line 13**) and on **Schedule SE, line 2**. (If you checked the box on line 1, see the line 31 instructions). Estates and trusts, enter on **Form 1041, line 3.** • If you checked 32b, you **must** attach **Form 6198.** Your loss may be limited.				32a ☐ All investment is at risk. 32b ☐ Some investment is not at risk.	

For Paperwork Reduction Act Notice, see the separate instructions.   Cat. No. 11334P   Schedule C (Form 1040 or 1040-SR) 2019

I'm a big believer that wealth can be built through the ownership of a business, so I hope that you one day have the opportunity to own or co-own a business.

Other forms that you may eventually need include Schedules B, D, and E.

Schedule B, Interest and Ordinary Dividends, is the first of these forms that I came across. Once I had money in savings accounts that started earning interest the bank reported that income to both me and to the IRS with Form 1099-INT Interest Income.

1099-INT Example

□ VOID □ CORRECTED		

PAYER'S name, street address, city or town, state or province, country, ZIP or foreign postal code, and telephone no.	Payer's RTN (optional)	OMB No. 1545-0112	
	1 Interest income $	**2020** Form **1099-INT**	**Interest Income**
	2 Early withdrawal penalty $		Copy 1
PAYER'S TIN RECIPIENT'S TIN	3 Interest on U.S. Savings Bonds and Treas. obligations $		For State Tax Department
RECIPIENT'S name	4 Federal income tax withheld $	5 Investment expenses $	
	6 Foreign tax paid $	7 Foreign country or U.S. possession	
Street address (including apt. no.)	8 Tax-exempt interest $	9 Specified private activity bond interest $	
City or town, state or province, country, and ZIP or foreign postal code	10 Market discount $	11 Bond premium $	
FATCA filing requirement □	12 Bond premium on Treasury obligations $	13 Bond premium on tax-exempt bond $	
Account number (see instructions)	14 Tax-exempt and tax credit bond CUSIP no.	15 State 16 State identification no. 17 State tax withheld $ $	

Form **1099-INT**   www.irs.gov/Form1099INT   Department of the Treasury - Internal Revenue Service

If you own shares of a company outside of a retirement account, you are likely to receive Form 1099-DIV, Dividends and Distributions, if the company pays dividends on that stock.

1099-DIV Example

□ VOID □ CORRECTED		

PAYER'S name, street address, city or town, state or province, country, ZIP or foreign postal code, and telephone no.	1a Total ordinary dividends $	OMB No. 1545-0110	
	1b Qualified dividends $	**2020** Form **1099-DIV**	**Dividends and Distributions**
	2a Total capital gain distr. $	2b Unrecap. Sec. 1250 gain $	Copy 1
PAYER'S TIN RECIPIENT'S TIN	2c Section 1202 gain $	2d Collectibles (28%) gain $	For State Tax Department
RECIPIENT'S name	3 Nondividend distributions $	4 Federal income tax withheld $	
	5 Section 199A dividends $	6 Investment expenses $	
Street address (including apt. no.)	7 Foreign tax paid $	8 Foreign country or U.S. possession	
City or town, state or province, country, and ZIP or foreign postal code	9 Cash liquidation distributions $	10 Noncash liquidation distributions $	
FATCA filing requirement □	11 Exempt-interest dividends $	12 Specified private activity bond interest dividends $	
Account number (see instructions)	13 State 14 State identification no.	15 State tax withheld $ $	

Form **1099-DIV**   www.irs.gov/Form1099DIV   Department of the Treasury - Internal Revenue Service

Both the 1099-INT and 1099-DIV are used to complete Schedule B.

Schedule B Example

Schedule E, Supplemental Income and Loss, is likely the next form you will come across. For me, I started to need Schedule E when I began investing in real estate. It is a convenient form to quickly input the rents and expenses for up to three properties[24] when you own the properties in either your own name or a single-member LLC[25].

Schedule E Example

SCHEDULE E
(Form 1040 or 1040-SR)
Department of the Treasury
Internal Revenue Service (99)

Supplemental Income and Loss
(From rental real estate, royalties, partnerships, S corporations, estates, trusts, REMICs, etc.)
► Attach to Form 1040, 1040-SR, 1040-NR, or 1041.
► Go to *www.irs.gov/ScheduleE* for instructions and the latest information.

OMB No. 1545-0074
2019
Attachment Sequence No. **13**

Name(s) shown on return

Your social security number

Part I — Income or Loss From Rental Real Estate and Royalties Note: If you are in the business of renting personal property, use Schedule C (see instructions). If you are an individual, report farm rental income or loss from Form 4835 on page 2, line 40.

A Did you make any payments in 2019 that would require you to file Form(s) 1099? (see instructions) . . . . . . ☐ Yes ☐ No
B If "Yes," did you or will you file required Forms 1099? . . . ☐ Yes ☐ No

1a Physical address of each property (street, city, state, ZIP code)

A

B

C

1b	Type of Property (from list below)	2 For each rental real estate property listed above, report the number of fair rental and personal use days. Check the QJV box only if you meet the requirements to file as a qualified joint venture. See instructions.		Fair Rental Days	Personal Use Days	QJV
A			A			☐
B			B			☐
C			C			☐

Type of Property:
1 Single Family Residence
2 Multi-Family Residence
3 Vacation/Short-Term Rental
4 Commercial
5 Land
6 Royalties
7 Self-Rental
8 Other (describe)

Income:	Properties:	A	B	C
3 Rents received	3			
4 Royalties received	4			
Expenses:				
5 Advertising	5			
6 Auto and travel (see instructions)	6			
7 Cleaning and maintenance	7			
8 Commissions.	8			
9 Insurance	9			
10 Legal and other professional fees	10			
11 Management fees	11			
12 Mortgage interest paid to banks, etc. (see instructions)	12			
13 Other interest.	13			
14 Repairs.	14			
15 Supplies	15			
16 Taxes	16			
17 Utilities.	17			
18 Depreciation expense or depletion	18			
19 Other (list) ► _____	19			
20 Total expenses. Add lines 5 through 19 . .	20			
21 Subtract line 20 from line 3 (rents) and/or 4 (royalties). If result is a (loss), see instructions to find out if you must file Form 6198	21			
22 Deductible rental real estate loss after limitation, if any, on Form 8582 (see instructions)	22	( )	( )	( )

23a Total of all amounts reported on line 3 for all rental properties 23a
  b Total of all amounts reported on line 4 for all royalty properties 23b
  c Total of all amounts reported on line 12 for all properties 23c
  d Total of all amounts reported on line 18 for all properties 23d
  e Total of all amounts reported on line 20 for all properties 23e

24 Income. Add positive amounts shown on line 21. Do not include any losses 24
25 Losses. Add royalty losses from line 21 and rental real estate losses from line 22. Enter total losses here . 25 ( )
26 Total rental real estate and royalty income or (loss). Combine lines 24 and 25. Enter the result here. If Parts II, III, IV, and line 40 on page 2 do not apply to you, also enter this amount on Schedule 1 (Form 1040 or 1040-SR), line 5, or Form 1040-NR, line 18. Otherwise, include this amount in the total on line 41 on page 2 26

For Paperwork Reduction Act Notice, see the separate instructions.   Cat. No. 11344L   Schedule E (Form 1040 or 1040-SR) 2019

---

[24] For more than three properties, you just keep adding more Schedule E forms. There is no limit.

[25] A *single member LLC* means you are the only owner of the company. Sometimes a husband and a wife as the only members (owners) of an LLC can still be considered a single member LLC. A single-member LLC is considered a disregarded entity for tax purposes, which allows the income and expenses to be reported directly on Schedule E versus the need to file its own tax return.

Page 2 of Schedule E is used when income is reported to you via Form K-1, Partner's Share of Income, Deductions, Credits, etc. See a bit further on for an example of Form K-1.

Schedule E (Form 1040 or 1040-SR) 2019

You receive a K-1 most commonly when you are a co-owner in an LLC, partnership, or corporation. When that entity has filed their own taxes, they provide this information to the IRS and need to report it to you for your own tax purposes.

K-1 Example

The last form important to be aware of is Schedule D, Capital Gains and Losses. As you begin to accumulate wealth, you will likely begin to invest in the stock market, real estate, or businesses. All of these are considered assets and the business itself will likely own assets inside of it, such as heavy equipment.

Using stocks as a simple example: If you buy a single share of stock in your own name (versus through a retirement account) for $100 and then sell it for $120, you have a Capital Gain of $20. If you held the stock for less than a year, it is considered a short-term gain; if you held it for more than a year, it is considered a long-term gain. That gain is considered income and is taxable. One reason that a lot of stock is held in retirement accounts is that these gains are ignored inside retirement accounts. That way, you don't have to constantly be paying capital gains taxes as you buy and sell stocks.

Schedule D Example

Filing Status

Before going any further, you should understand the five basic types of filing statuses:

- **Single** – an unmarried person filing a tax return.
- **Married Filing Jointly** – a married couple who are filing a tax return together.
- **Head of Household** – an unmarried person who maintains a home for a qualifying person. The most common type of qualifying person is your child whom you claim as a dependent, but other relatives may also meet this qualification.
- **Married Filing Separately** – a married couple that chooses to file separate tax returns.
- **Qualifying Widow/Widower** – After the loss of a spouse, you may continue to receive the tax benefits of the Married Filing Jointly status for up to two years. You must have a dependent child to qualify and not re-marry in that time.

Deductions and Credits

A tax **deduction** lowers your tax liability by offsetting your income. You can reduce the amount of taxes you have to pay by lowering your total taxable income through deductions. Typical tax deductions include home mortgage interest expense, healthcare costs, property taxes, and casualty or theft losses.

To claim most tax deductions, you have to complete Schedule A. This is called **itemizing deductions**. Schedule A walks you through listing your deductions. However, there are a few caveats.

First, you can deduct only those medical expenses that exceed 10 percent[26] of your adjusted gross income. So, if you make $50,000 per year, your medical expenses need to exceed $5,000, and only the amount over that is deductible.

Second, all tax filers[27] are eligible to claim a **standard deduction** first rather than itemize deductions at all. As of 2019, a single person has a standard deduction of $12,200.[28] Your deductions on Schedule A must

---

[26] As of 2020. Previously it was 7.50 percent.

[27] Unless you are Married Filing Separately, and your spouse uses Schedule A to itemize their deductions.

[28] Married Filing Jointly have a $24,400 standard deduction as does a Qualifying Widow/Widower. Head of Household has a standard deduction of $18,350.

exceed the standard deduction for it to have any impact on your taxes. Since the time I started filing taxes at sixteen, I have not yet filed Schedule A.

Schedule A Example

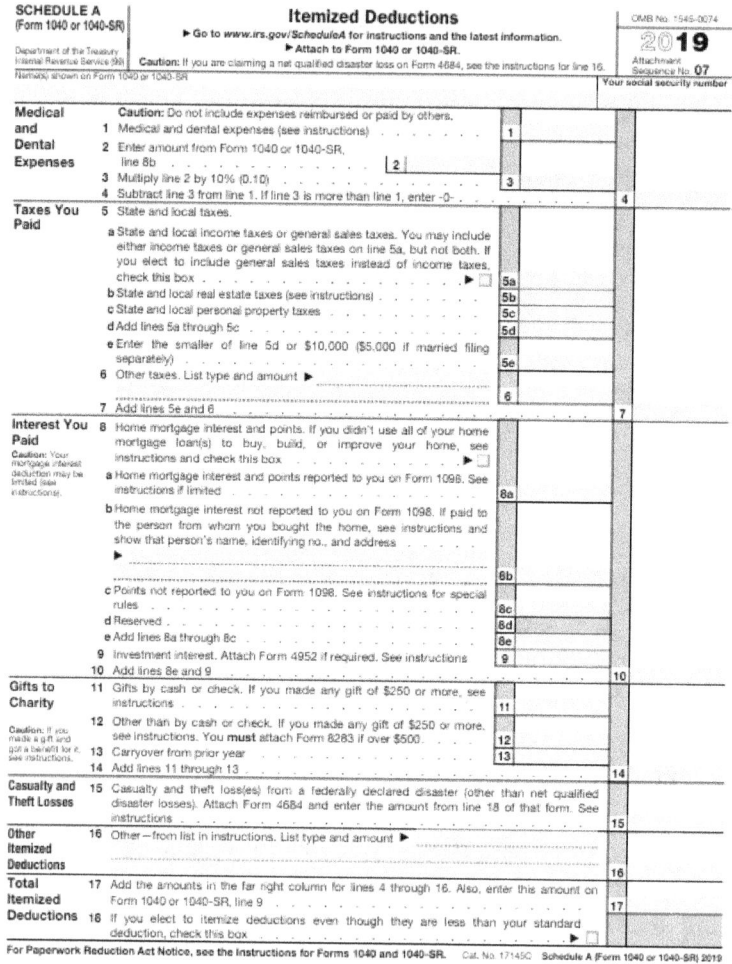

Aside from deductions, there are also credits. A tax **credit** does not lower your taxable income but instead directly offsets any taxes you owe.

A **refundable credit** is one that is used to offset any income taxes you owe first, and if the credit exceeds the amount of taxes owed, you receive the difference back. The earned income credit, the child tax credit, and part of the

American opportunity credit are examples of this type of credit.

A **non-refundable credit** is one that can be used to offset any income taxes owed, but if the amount of the credit exceeds taxes owed, you do not receive any money back, and the rest of the credit is lost. Common examples of this type of credit are the child and dependent care credit, the lifetime learning credit, and the residential energy efficient property credit.

The key point I want to make about tax deductions and credits is that most of them require you to either have spent or lost money. Deductions such as healthcare costs, property taxes, and mortgage interest are mostly deductible but require you to have spent money as opposed to the earned income credit, which is not tied to money you've spent. Credits for childcare or energy efficient upgrades to your home also require that you have spent money in exchange for them. The child tax credit and the earned income credit are some of the few credits that don't require money to have been spent by you in order to obtain them. However, the child tax credit does require that you have children (which costs money), and the earned income credit is designed to help people with low-to-moderate incomes so the more successful you become the less likely you will be able to receive it.

Benefits to Owning Businesses and Real Estate Investments

There are many benefits to owning a business and real estate investments but I'm going to talk about only the potential tax benefits here.

Filing Schedule C or Schedule E (see above) allows you to take depreciation. **Depreciation** is when you take the cost of an asset such as a computer or a building and spread the cost of it across several years on your taxes. A computer may last you five years in a business, so you split up the cost of the computer and allocate a portion (typically an equal portion) for each year. A building can be depreciated over 27.5 years, as they last much longer than a computer.

In some cases, you can use **Section 179 Depreciation Deduction,** which allows you to fully depreciate an asset in the year you acquire it. If you buy a truck for $20,000 for your business, you can expense the whole $20,000 in the first year. This lowers your income in the business by $20,000 (compared to just $4,000) if you were to depreciate it over five years.[29]

---

[29] There are a lot of concerns related to this when you finance a vehicle and the impact it has on your cashflow compared to the income you state to the IRS. Be

If your business or real estate investment generates a loss (took in less money than the expenses you had), the loss offsets any other income you report on your 1040 tax return.

What You Should Look for in Your Tax Professional

A tax professional is often an accountant but can also be a highly skilled bookkeeper that has obtained a PTIN (Preparer Tax Identification Number). Either way, a tax professional should have the education necessary to complete most tax returns.

When I first decided I needed to stop doing my own taxes and get the help of a professional, I was working as a commercial lender. During my career up to that point, I had interacted with several accountants, as I worked through income information with clients.

I figured I had an advantage in choosing an accountant, because I could see which businesses were doing well and who their accountants were. I noticed a trend and set up an appointment to meet with a member of that firm.

During the initial consultation,[30] the accountant seemed knowledgeable, but she was somewhat aloof. We didn't connect on a personal level. I didn't get a bad feeling about her. I just didn't get *any* feeling about her. After meeting with her for an hour, I didn't know anything about her other than her name and her appearing to be about my age. Also, she was an accountant and worked for the firm I thought was one of the best in the city.

The first year, things went smoothly. The second year, I had some changes to my income and asked for advice halfway through the year. I feel that mid-year meeting went poorly. I don't think she grasped all the changes I was making, and as a result, I underpaid my taxes enough to have a minor penalty for underpayment. Furthermore, when the time came to do my taxes, she made a rather sizeable mistake that I didn't catch for a few months. We were able to re-file and get some money back later, but the mistake shouldn't have happened. All of this was on top of the fact that I was paying a premium

---

sure to speak with an accountant and a business advisor/mentor when considering using this.

[30] An initial consultation is usually a free meeting during which you can get to know each other. You see whether their skills will satisfy your needs, while they feel you out to get an idea of your situation.

price for the services being rendered.

Following this awful second year, I decided to switch accounting firms. By then, I had more contacts in the industry. I discussed my taxes with people at two different companies that I had come to know. Both were knowledgeable, and I had connected with both on a personal level before even discussing the option of having them work for me. I ended up choosing one that was younger because I felt her practice was more in line with where I was in life and where I wanted to go. Also, I was concerned about the older one retiring.[31]

Once you get to the point of hiring a tax professional, I think you should talk to at least two or three before making your final decision. If you don't have a good feeling about any of the ones you talk to, find a few more to choose from. Don't be afraid to set up a follow-up meeting with them if you are uncertain. If they want your business, they will agree to it.

Accountants, bookkeepers, and other tax professionals are not known for their people skills. Don't be surprised if they come across as cold, aloof, or weird, though you do have to get beyond this in order to feel comfortable with them. They are going to be handling a lot of your personal sensitive information.

As part of getting comfortable with them, you want to make sure that their practice aligns with what you are doing in life and that they will be able to provide you with good advice for several years (maybe decades). They should have a lot of knowledge on situations similar to yours. If you are building your 5th business and planning an IPO[32] next year, you probably don't want an accountant that specializes in helping medical professionals that work for the local hospital. Be prepared to interviewing them along with sharing information about yourself and your situation to see whether the two of you will fit well together. Below are some questions you can ask. They are meant to be a guideline to help you get comfortable with the person, but they are not set in stone.

---

[31] When I first started looking for accountants, the first person I felt comfortable with and approached told me he was in his final year and then was retiring.

[32] IPO stands for Initial Public Offering. It is a way for businesses to sell stock in the business to raise money and for the founding investors/partners to cash in on some of their hard work. IPO places shares of the company for sale on a stock market exchange and allows the general public to purchase and sell shares without the management of the company being involved.

- How long have you been an accountant (or tax professional)?
- What types of clients do you work with most?
- Do you have experience helping people in situations similar to mine? (Be prepared to describe your situation.)
- Other than yourself, will anyone else be working on my file? If so, what is their knowledge and experience level? How much will they be involved?
- How do you structure your appointments during tax season? Will I get a packet to fill out each year?
- If they are necessary, how do you handle tax extensions?
- What are your current rates for tax preparation and for any advisor meetings throughout the year?
- Any other fees or costs that I should be aware of?
- Do you have any concerns about having me as a client?
- Is there anything else I should know about working with you?

Other Common Tax Terms

- Tax Bracket – Depending on your income, you fall into a "tax bracket." These are percentages of income taxes charged based on income ranges. In 2019, the tax rate for single filers making less than $9,700 was 10 percent; $9,701–$39,475, 12 percent; $39,476–$84,200, 22 percent; $84,201–$160,725, 24 percent; $160,726–$204,100, 32 percent; $204,101–$510,300, 35 percent; and $510,301 or more, 37percent.
- Refund – If you have overpaid your taxes throughout the year or receive refundable tax credits, you get that money back in the form of a refund.
- IRS – This stands for Internal Revenue Service, and they oversee all tax returns and collecting tax money due for the government. They can't make tax law, but they are in charge of reading the tax laws passed by the United States Congress and deciding how those laws are to be enforced.
- AGI – This stands for Adjusted Gross Income. This takes your total income less deductions like student loan interest or losses in a business. This is the number that tax rates are based on. This number is also often used by mortgage professionals to help you qualify for a home loan.

- Progressive Tax – The United States has a progressive tax. This means that the more money you earn in a year the greater the percent of that income goes to pay income taxes is (see Tax Bracket on previous page). This is so that low-income earners struggling to earn enough money to live on pay very little taxes, while high-income earners make up for them by paying more.
- Flat Tax – This has circulated as a theory for years, as some people think it would be better if the U.S. had only one tax bracket and all people paid the same percentage of their income in taxes. A flat tax of 20 percent would mean that whether you earned $10 or a million dollars, you would pay 20 percent (or $2 and $200,000). Compare this to a progressive tax, when the $10 earner would pay $1 and the one million earner would pay $370,000 (per the 2019 tax bracket listed above). A flat tax would be a great deal for people making a lot of money but would place a larger burden on people earning very little who need every penny they earn to live off of.

State Tax Returns

On top of completing a federal tax return and submitting it to the IRS, you will also likely need to complete a state tax return. Each state has its own government system that exists separate from the U.S. national government. In order to have their own money to spend, states have to collect taxes also. There are a few states that do not have income taxes and don't require a tax return to be completed, but most do. The states that don't are likely to rely more on sales tax (taxes on everyday things you buy) and property taxes (taxes paid every year for a home or other real estate that you own).

Each state is different, so it would be overwhelming to put them all in here. However, most states base their tax returns on information you complete on Form 1040. The directions are likely to ask you to pull your adjusted gross income (AGI) from the 1040 and then fill out the rest of the state tax form.

State tax forms are often much shorter than the federal forms. You can often find free ways to file them just like you can for simple Form 1040. Most online services have state-filing options.

Free Services

If you get the chance, take a class on tax preparation. I was taught by my parents how to fill out my first tax returns by hand. I then took a tax preparation class from Liberty Tax, which walked us through filling out more complicated tax returns by hand before ever touching a computer. Learning how to do it by hand, rather than just answering questions on a computer, made me understand the process much more. Many communities offer free tax classes at libraries and community centers. Liberty Tax offers a class with the only cost being the book. At the end of the class, they recruit top students to work for them.

Aside from free and cheap classes, you can often find free tax preparation services offered by local colleges. Colleges with accounting classes offer these services for their students to get hands-on experience preparing tax returns. Other community organizations often offer free tax preparation as well.

If you are computer savvy, you can find resources online to fill out tax returns for free. Some of the big companies like TurboTax and H&R Block allow users to fill out basic tax returns for free. The IRS also has free software, which you can use to do your taxes, and links to free state return options as well.

If you have the patience, you can find the forms to fill out on the IRS's website and download them to complete them by hand. Sometimes local libraries also have copies of the forms for free or for sale at minimal prices. All the forms include directions, and you can find further directions online by googling them.

Many of the free options are limited by income or complexity. Also, make sure you look over any tax returns that have been prepared for you and ensure that the information is accurate before you sign it and send it in, which is one more reason you should learn about what you are looking at by taking a class.

Why I Want My Daughter to Know This

I once heard that if you don't want to pay taxes, then don't make any money. This is a terrible mindset that I have seen countless people adopt. Personally, I'd rather owe the IRS a ton of money, because that means I'm making even more money. I'm going to use every deduction I can in order to minimize what I owe them, but I'd still rather make money than lose money.

It is important to understand basic tax preparation lingo and principles so you can intelligently converse with a tax preparer or know what you are doing when preparing your own taxes.

It's also important to understand that you obtain most tax deductions and credits by spending or losing money.

I want my daughter to know how to prepare her own taxes, and I want her to know that when her situation grows big enough she should seek professional assistance. Most of all, I want her to understand that paying taxes can be painful, but it is also a measure of your success.

Lastly, I think it is important to have a basic understanding of taxes so that you can (and you should) review the work of your tax preparer and check it for errors. Had I reviewed one of my tax returns better, I would have caught the mistake the accountant had made earlier and wouldn't have had to re-file and wait for money back.

9: IS COLLEGE RIGHT FOR YOU AND HOW TO PAY FOR IT

"Dad, I know what I want to be when I grow up!"

"Oh yeah? What is that?"

"I want to be a veterinarian and work with animals."

"That's great," I said. "I think you would be very good at it. Have you really thought about it?"

"Yes. I know it requires more college, but I think I should be able to afford it. I will do as many college classes in high school as I can. Then maybe go to a community college before transferring to a university to get a bachelor's degree and then go on for my advanced degree. If I can get scholarship help also, I will do that too."

"I can tell you've put a lot of thought into how to achieve this already."

"Yes. I think it will be fun to work with animals all day."

"I think so too. What types of animals do you want to work with?"

"Dogs and cats and other pets."

"You know there is a large demand for vets on dairy farms and cattle ranches."

"I know. But Granddad told me the cows sometimes poop on him when he has to do pregnancy checks. So I don't want to do that."

I laughed. "That's true. But there are downsides to working with pets also."

"The poop is smaller."

I laughed again. "True, but have you really thought about all the downsides?"

"Yes."

"So you are aware that you will be working with a lot of animals that are sick."

"Yes."

"And that some of those animals may die?"

"Yes," Ashla replied a bit less enthusiastically.

"And that sometimes you may have to put them down?"

Horror crossed over my daughter's face as the implications dawned on her. "I don't want to be a vet anymore."

College isn't right for everyone. I didn't think it was right for me, so I hadn't planned on going. I delayed going to the Navy for a year so I could at least try out college at the request of my mother. I went on only two college tours, one of which I had attended because it included a seminar on leadership. I decided on the college I would go to because a friend of mine was going there. Not exactly the best way to go about deciding to attend college and which one to attend.

Looking back, it was one of the best experiences of my life. It was where I met my wife. I also had an absolute blast during my freshman year. Parties weren't really my thing, but I did go to a few. I really enjoyed the social life that accompanied dorm living. But these are also not reasons to attend college.

After I had been discharged from the Navy, I went back and finished college because I didn't know what else I should be doing with my life. I had no direction. My wife wanted to be a teacher and needed a degree to do that. I went back because she was going back. I was so directionless that I ended up taking several of the PE classes that she took for her Physical Education major. As a result, I graduated with 12 PE credits, while needing only one.

Once I had finished college, I didn't know what I wanted to do. Attending college career fairs didn't really help me, because nothing sounded interesting. I bounced around among a lot of different jobs that didn't require college education.

I ended up as a teller at a bank and worked my way up to be a commercial lender. As a result, I was never once asked about my college education while in any job interview. Once I had established myself as a commercial lender, potential employers were more interested in my experience than my education. Maybe having a college education got me through the door, but I don't know for certain, as they never brought it up during the interview.

I'm a perfect example of someone who shouldn't have gone to college. I should have just entered the workforce and started earning better money earlier. I also could have avoided the costs of college and the debt. My wife and I both worked as much as we could and paid for most of our college via scholarships, grants, or money we earned. However, grants and scholarships began to dry up during our junior year. We had our daughter that year as well, which limited the time we could spend working. As a result, our senior year was more costly and ended up plunging us into student debt.

Straight into the Workforce

Many argue that there aren't a whole lot of opportunities for young people with just a high school diploma. I would counter that there aren't very many more opportunities available by obtaining a generalized college degree.

Without a college degree, you immediately have a blank spot on your resume; however, you can spend four years building your resume while earning money rather than four years spending money (you don't have) to obtain a degree.

The biggest advantages of going straight into the workforce are the immediate income you will be receiving and the college debt you will be avoiding. Should you decide to get a degree later, you always can.

Without a college degree, you may be limited in your career choices but still have many options. You can get a job in many fields, doing manual labor (such as farming) or various construction jobs. Service work such as serving at a restaurant, working for a hotel, or in a call center may not be the most glamorous, but many people still make careers out of them. You can also join the military, which offers tons of career paths, decent pay, good benefits, and opportunities to complete college classes. Lastly, you could start your own business at a time in your life when you have a ton of energy and low living expenses if you are still living with your parents.

Technical Schools

I'm a big proponent of technical schools. You can learn a trade in a short amount of time, and the annual cost is typically less than that of a university. Some of the careers that can be quickly learned include welders, automotive mechanics, nurses/dental assistants, and commercial pilots. These programs can all be completed in less than four years, some less than two years, and they are all in demand and pay well.

Community College or Junior College

Community college and junior college are terms that are sometimes used interchangeably. Both are designed to catch students who did not perform as well academically in high school. Often, they have a lot of preparatory classes that allow students to build skills and obtain credit hours before transferring on to universities. Both types of colleges also offer associate degree programs and certificate programs. Some of them are also geared as technical schools.

Most commonly, educators have described community colleges as a place where students can live at home and attend classes. Whereas many junior colleges offer dorms, and students can move to the school to attend classes. In Northern Colorado, close to where I live, there is AIMS Community College (https://www.aims.edu/) and Northeastern Junior College (https://www.njc.edu/).

If you are planning to attend a community or junior college and then transfer to a university, you should check and make sure the credit hours[33] you are obtaining will transfer. Not all do. AIMS works closely with the University of Northern Colorado, so most of their credit hours transfer.

College in High School

I had a lot of fun in high school and took a lot of classes that I thought were interesting. However, I didn't take advantage of any college-level classes, mostly because I wasn't planning on attending college.

AP (Advanced Placement) and IB (International Baccalaureate) are two programs that allow students to complete college-level programs and obtain credit hours for classes while still in high school. These are widely accepted across universities. I did take an AP World History course while I was in high school, because I love history. I got bored and dropped it halfway through the year, so I didn't get college credit for it. Because of this, I had to take a history class when I went to college. I have to say that the college history class was much easier than the AP class.

Some schools are now starting to offer dual enrollment. Typically, these are courses offered at a local college and are taught either at the college or at the high school if there is enough demand. These classes can replace classes found in high school and allow students to finish both high school and college courses at the same time. This may allow a student to avoid many or all of the costly college enrollment fees.

A different structure is concurrent enrollment. This is an option for students that have exhausted the school's available courses in a particular subject. The student can enroll into the college to complete additional courses

---

[33] Credit hours are the unit of tracking completion of class requirements in college. A college may require you to have six credit hours in English and need to take two English classes worth three credits each in order fulfill this requirement.

in that subject. These courses are rarely taught at the high school level and require the student to attend the college. Most commonly, these courses are offered through a community college. Concurrent enrollment is very similar to dual enrollment. It may also help students avoid costly enrollment fees.

Another option is to enroll directly into college classes during summer sessions. College summer classes are fast paced but can allow students to knock out credit hours quickly. This requires students to enroll directly into the college, and there are likely to be enrollment fees as a result.

For-Profit Schools

I am very wary of for-profit schools (as opposed to state-run not-for-profit schools). The incentive at a for-profit school is to make money, and they make money by only increasing enrollment. Therefore, they let in a lot of students who may not be college appropriate and keep them enrolled and paying money, even though the students probably should fail out.

However, some for-profit schools fill a niche that state-run schools can't fill. An example of this is commercial piloting schools. It is very difficult for state-run schools to operate any sort of piloting programs. Hence, a rise in private schools offering these programs.

If you are considering attending any sort of for-profit school, you should do your research. Is the school accredited? Being accredited is a quality assurance program that means the school meets or exceeds a minimum standard of quality. Schools that are accredited are helpful if you decide to transfer, because the credit hours (classes) you've completed are more likely to transfer.

Does the school offer a placement program? Are the students graduating from the school able to obtain jobs in the careers they are being trained for? These are just a couple questions that can help you evaluate whether the school is legitimate.

State University

State universities, sometimes referred to as public universities, capture the majority of college-bound students. The typical model is a four-year track that results in a bachelor's degree in a specific field of study. State universities have dorms for on-campus living but usually have off-campus housing options for students once they move beyond their first year.

Living in on-campus housing can be more expensive than living in off-campus housing and usually requires students to also participate in a mandatory meal plan with campus dining halls, which also can increase expenses.

Universities usually have sports teams, numerous social clubs revolving around a wide variety of interests, and Greek fraternities and sororities.

Many state universities will help you automatically apply for any state-sponsored scholarships at the same time you enroll. This helps them secure funding and reduces the cost to you.

Private University

The biggest difference between a private university and a public/state university is how they are funded. Public and state institutions receive money from the government to cover some of their costs. Private universities don't receive those funds and have to rely on tuition and donations to cover their costs. Keep in mind when paying full price that private universities are often much more expensive than their state-run counterparts. However, because private universities receive a lot of donations and typically have endowments,[34] it is possible for students to receive sizable scholarships to help pay for their tuition. There are a lot of big name private colleges such as Harvard, MIT, and Stanford. Private universities tend to have higher admissions standard, which perpetuates their elite status.

Private universities often share a lot of activities that state universities support, such as sports teams, clubs, and Greek life.

---

[34] An endowment is a set of funds that have been donated and are earmarked for certain things such as scholarships. This money is typically invested, and the return it receives is used to fund scholarships or other programs.

Ways to Pay for College

- LESS EXPENSIVE COLLEGES – If you have decided to go to college, one of the easiest ways to keep costs down is to go to a less expensive college. If you were looking at a private university such as Harvard, Stanford, or maybe a local one such as the University of Denver, you may want to look at state colleges that offer similar programs and compare the costs. You may be able to get the same education for less cost.
- IN-STATE TUITION – Colleges and universities love charging out-of-state residents more than in-state residents, because they can. People going to school in other states are likely to have more resources (money) than those attending in-state schools and are better able to afford it. You can keep your costs down by attending a school in the state you live. Some universities extend in-state tuition to neighboring states. Others have sister universities in other states that you can transfer to after a semester or two and receive in-state pricing. Another strategy is to move to the state where you want to attend college and live there for a year, establishing residency. Then you can enroll at in-state pricing.
- SCHOLARSHIPS – Getting someone else to foot the bill while you are in college is excellent. Some scholarships are awarded directly by the university to athletes, band members, or other types of students they are actively trying to recruit (see chapter 1 as to why it is important to participate and do well in activities). Other scholarships may be awarded by unrelated organizations that are trying to promote higher education among particular groups. Scholarships typically require an application and sometimes an essay. I have always heard that scholarship award committees like when people are active in their communities and volunteer (see chapter 1 again). When searching for scholarships, the two best resources are Google and your school guidance counselor. Additionally, if you are involved in organizations, it is a good idea to ask your network about any scholarships they are aware of, as there are many social organizations that have funds that go unused because they aren't advertised on the Internet.
- GRANTS – A grant is similar to a scholarship. But while a scholarship is based on merit, a grant is based on need. You should complete the Free Application for Federal Student Aid (FAFSA) as

early as you can. The FAFSA usually becomes available in January of each year and applies to the next upcoming school year. So you would fill it out while still a senior in high school. You're required to fill it out each year to obtain funds for the next year. You want to fill it out as early as possible, as some states and/or schools have limited funds that are allocated on a first-come-first-served basis. The process requires you to have your (and your parents') tax information available, as much of the aid is based on need. In addition to grants, the FAFSA will also tell you whether you qualify for some work study and federal student loan options.

- WORK STUDY – A work study is a job working for the college you are attending. You qualify for a work study opportunity through the FAFSA, as the college pays a portion of your wages, while the federal government pays another portion. While this doesn't directly pay for tuition, it does allow you to earn money while in college. The work study I obtained was designed to let me do menial office work part time and do schoolwork in my free time. This also helped me build my resume. I have heard of others who have had similar experiences.

- EMPLOYER REIMBURSEMENT AND TUITION ASSISTANCE – Many employers have programs that help their employees pay for college. Tuition assistance helps students up front to pay for the costs of college. Employer Reimbursement pays the student back some or all of the costs of courses once they are successfully completed. Each employer has its own rules. McDonald's has a generous program that requires you to be in good standing at the store you work at and will cover tuition and fees up to $2,500.[35] One bank I worked at encouraged us to enroll in special banking school courses and paid for all costs up front. We were required to repay the amount if we failed the course. Another bank I worked at would pay all costs at any approved school so long as the coursework was related to your career at the bank[36] and the employee signed a loan for seven years. Each year, the bank would forgive a portion of the loan. If the employee left early, they would then be required to make payments on the remaining balance of the loan.

---

[35] At the time of this writing, the $2,500 is available to non-manager franchise-owned employees, but they have more programs available to all their employees, http://www.archwaystoopportunity.com/tuition_assistance.html.
[36] Finance, accounting, business, economics, etc.

- WORKING AND SAVINGS – My wife and I both worked the entire time we were in college to help pay costs. My wife had some money saved up from working in high school, which also helped her pay for college. I would strongly encourage a portion of any earnings made in high school to be saved for college if that is the planned path. It is the time when your personal expenses are minimal and you can earn without needing to spend. Working through college can drastically reduce your need to pull on other financial resources.

- PARENTAL HELP – Many parents feel that it is their responsibility to pay for the children's college education. I feel the same. However, parents should first ensure their own financial needs are being met, including maxing out retirement savings. You can borrow money for college, but you can't borrow money for retirement. Once parents have maxed out their retirement savings, they can pay directly for college. Or with some pre-planning, they can use college savings plans such as a 529 plan or Coverdell ESA (Education Savings Account). Both of these accounts allow the money saved to grow tax free as long as the money is used for qualifying education expenses.

  o A 529 college savings plan allows beneficiaries[37] of any age to withdraw money for college expenses. There are no income restrictions to this plan, but contributions are limited to $14,000 per year.

  o Money in an ESA must be used by the beneficiary and can be used for expenses in primary and secondary school (elementary, middle, and high school) not just for college expenses. Contributions are limited to $2,000 per year, and the ability to contribute to an ESA phases out.[38]

- STUDENT LOANS – Loans are listed last because they should be a last resort. They are ridiculously easy to get, which makes them desirable (I know from experience). If you can not find other ways to pay for college, student loans can be obtained. I recommend student loans offered through the FAFSA first, as the terms, rates, and deferment options make them less cumbersome. Student loans offered through lenders such as banks are less friendly on all marks,

---

[37] A beneficiary is someone whom the account is set up for. Typically, a parent sets this up for their child, so the beneficiary would be the child.

[38] Currently, the phase-out is between $95,000 and $110,000 for single filers and between $190,000 and $200,000 for married filing jointly filers.

but they may be your only option in instances such as pursuing a commercial pilots license through a for-profit school.

Delayed College

Choosing not to go to college can be a great decision. You may also decide that you want to go later. Perhaps you want to work a few years and figure out what you want to pursue. It is also a way to build some savings in order to help pay for college. Perhaps you never intend to go to college, and then five or ten years later you change your mind.

My favorite benefit for delaying college is that it gives you a chance to figure out what you want to do. My first two years of college, I wanted to study political science and sociology. I took several classes of both and enjoyed them a lot. Midway through my sophomore year, my priorities shifted and I got this desire to learn about business. This was, in large part, due to the fact that many successful people I knew were business owners, not politicians or sociologists. I spent the next two years with a heavier-than-expected course load to catch up and graduate close to on time. In addition to a heavier course load, I also started taking a lot of summer school courses. I knocked out four courses between my sophomore and junior years, and another four between my junior and senior years. At the end of my fourth year, I still had one class left and finished that up in a summer course to finish my degree in August.[39]

My college life would have been a lot easier had I known from the beginning what path I wanted to pursue. As a result, I ended up with 154 credit hours at the time of graduation when I needed only 120. I had more than a year of extra classes that didn't help me graduate. That is a lot of time that I could have saved had I had a clear direction in the first place.

Delaying college can help you save money. It may also enable you to get qualified for an employer tuition assistance plan. Many require you to work for the employer for a while before you qualify.

However, choosing to delay college does have negatives. You may no

---

[39] This occurred while my wife and I both worked 40+ hours a week while raising our newborn daughter for the last year and a half. We couldn't afford daycare, so we worked and went to school on opposite schedules. We saw each other less than five hours a day, and those five hours were usually spent sleeping. On Thursday–Sunday, my mother helped watching Ashla, which allowed us to both work and/or attend classes at the same time. It gave us a crash course in time management.

longer qualify or have access to as many scholarships and grants. They are still out there, but they may be harder to come by.

It is also socially isolating when you attend classes with people even just a year younger than yourself. I was out of college for a year during my Navy adventure. When I came back, I was in classes with friends of mine that had graduated a year behind me in high school. Also, I was married by that point and found it difficult to relate to others. It was hard to just go hang out with people. This was before Facebook, so I lost track of a lot of the people I had known before. If you are a very social person, delaying college may feel more awkward when you do return.

Why I Want My Daughter to Know This

Starting at around the time of Ashla's 12th birthday, we began seriously discussing with her the subject of life after high school. Not just "whom she wanted to be when she grew up" but all the intricacies of getting there. This meant discussing college *and* ways of paying for it.

My daughter should have every tool available to pay for college before she needs to take on student debt. She should be able to make a decision that balances all of her life goals, not just her college goals.

It's crazy that we let people who have had very little financial responsibility up to this point in their lives take on such massive student debt. After all, the time it takes to pay back this debt is longer than the number of years they have been alive. Most have had no debt whatsoever up until this point, and suddenly they can sign up for loans that exceed their earnings up to then.

I will do everything I can to help my daughter avoid student loans. In the end, if she chooses to go to a private university without receiving financial aid or to pursue advanced degrees, the cost may exceed what I am able or willing to help her with. When that point comes, she needs to be educated enough to realize the impact on the rest of her life that taking on student debt will have.

Then, if she complains about student debt later in life, at least I can say, "I told you so."

10: GETTING A CAR

"Did you get a car when you turned sixteen?" Ashla asked me.

"Yes, I did."

"Did you have to pay for it?"

"No, my parents gave it to me."

"Cool! What type of car was it?"

"It was an eighteen-year-old Honda Accord. They had bought it a year earlier for $1,000, and my mother drove it for a year before it became mine. They planned from the beginning for it to be mine, and my mother got another vehicle when I turned sixteen."

"Are you getting me a car when I turn sixteen?" Ashla asked. She was thirteen, in middle school, and saw high schoolers driving every day.

"We've already got it," I replied. "You are getting Mom's old car. That's why we just got her a new car."

She wasn't exactly thrilled about this but seemed to accept the idea. She thought about it for a minute. "Why?"

"Why are we giving you a car or why are we giving you that one?" I asked for clarification.

"I guess both."

"We are giving you that one because we already own it. If we sold it, we would probably get $500 to $1,000 for it. Then, if we were to get you a car in a couple of years, we would be looking at paying $1,000 or more for a car that we thought was as reliable as this car has been. We know this car and what it's capable of. It's not very fast and doesn't have a lot of power, so we aren't too worried about your racing it around. It's also old enough, so no one will be upset about the car getting destroyed if you do get in an accident.

"As for why we are getting you a car," I continued, "We know that you are a trustworthy person. We've seen it in you for years. We know that you will make good choices and that you will call us for help if you get into trouble. My parents got me a car for the same reason. They trusted me. It's not that they didn't trust my friends, but they knew they couldn't control whose car I would get into unless they gave me a car."

"That makes sense. Do you think any of my friends will get cars?"

"God, I hope not. I've met your friends. We're getting you a car because we don't trust them."

My first rule of getting a car is don't do it until you have to. Getting a car is cool. I thought I was hot stuff when I got my first car—a 1982 Honda Accord. I was 16 and one of the few in my circle of friends to get a car from their parents. My car was old and prone to breaking down, but it gave me a level of freedom I hadn't had up until that point.

My wife didn't get her first car until after we were married. She didn't get her driver's license until after we were engaged and got it only because she wanted to come out and see me after boot camp. Her mother would take her to and from school and work. When she wanted to do something else, one of her friends or another (most of whom had cars) was happy to give her a ride.

I was on my second car, a VW Jetta, by the time we got married. The old Honda had lasted for about a year before it needed a new transmission, which was going to cost more than my parents had paid for the car. My wife and I shared that car for a couple of years. At one point, my mother gave me her old car, but we drove it so rarely that the battery was always dead.

We finally replaced the Jetta after the birth of our daughter. We bought a Scion Xb and sold off the Jetta. It was habit for us to share a vehicle. Our lives revolved around only needing one vehicle. Rebecca worked less than a mile from our house, college was less than a mile away, and my work was only four miles away. A lot of time, we walked or rode our bikes to get where we needed to go.

We got an old truck at one point so we could do work on our rentals. We used that truck a lot but rarely drove it to work, and it would often have a dead battery from lack of use as well. We finally got rid of the truck when it became too expensive to fix the emissions problems.

We did end up getting a small Yamaha Scooter a couple of years later. We ended up putting more miles on the scooter than we put on our car that year. It got great gas mileage, so we used it the most. The problem with the scooter was that we could only get around town with it.

Then I got a job that was out of town. While it was only three miles away, it was across a narrow bridge with a speed limit of 50 mph. The scooter couldn't go that fast, so I transitioned to riding a bike a lot. My wife then got a job that required her to drive all over the county, so the scooter began to sit idle most of the time.

We used just the Scion Xb and a bike for about three more years until I began working as a commercial lender, and it required me to go out and meet people where they worked. Finally, we purchased a second car that we could keep running. We'd been married for eleven years before it became necessary for both of us to have a car all the time.

Uber and Lyft didn't become available until a few years after that. But if they had been around, I might have been able to put off buying a car for another year or two. Both services are inexpensive ways to get around, and I would have been able to pay for several trips a month instead of the car payment, insurance, and maintenance costs that went into my vehicle.

Leasing vs. Buying

Leasing a vehicle is just renting it for a predetermined number of years. I don't like leasing vehicles. If you exceed your mileage limit, you are charged more. Often, it still requires a down payment. Your payments are sometimes a little bit cheaper than if you were buying it, but you never own the vehicle.

Leasing makes sense only if you are the type of person that wants a new vehicle every few years. If you are that type of person, you probably aren't going to listen to much of the advice given in this book. Since you are trading in the vehicle every couple of years, your maintenance costs are lower, as you are always under the factory warranty.

Purchasing a car allows you to get into a used vehicle that is less expensive. When choosing a new vehicle, you often can get no/low down payment options. The interest rates available on new vehicles are very low so long as you have good credit (see Chapter 6 on Credit). Once you have the loan paid off, you can continue to drive the vehicle without a monthly payment.

One downside of owning a vehicle is that if you purchased a used one, you may not have a warranty on it, so your maintenance costs are higher. Also, if you finance it for a long time, the warranty may expire before the loan is paid off. A warranty is a promise from the car company to repair certain items if they break before a set time period or distance. A bumper-to-bumper warranty includes most items. A powertrain or drivetrain warranty usually covers only the engine and other mechanical parts. A rust or corrosion warranty covers repairs due to rust. (This one is more important in different parts of the country. Where I live, it is dry and rust isn't a big deal).

When you want to sell the vehicle, you can trade it in at a dealership and get some credit towards a different vehicle; however, often you can get more money for it by selling it yourself. This can be a hassle. On the bright side, the continued growth of Craigslist and Facebook Marketplace have made it easier to get in front of more potential buyers.

New vs. Old

When buying a car, you can choose whether you want to buy a brand new car or a used one. Brand new cars are very nice, but they are more expensive. Cars depreciate, meaning they go down in value the longer they are driven.[40] The worst depreciation hit in a car's life is the day it is driven off the lot. The moment you buy it, a new car is worth less than you paid for it.

There is a lot of peace of mind that comes with purchasing a new car. You know that it hasn't been in any accidents. No one else has owned it and driven it hard. You don't have to worry about how well it's been maintained. New cars also come with a factory warranty that covers a lot of the maintenance that a car could need over the first few years. Often, dealerships will throw in oil changes for the first couple of years as an incentive for you to buy a car from them, which further reduces your maintenance costs.

Most of the time, financing (the loan you can get) on a new vehicle is less expensive. Some dealerships even offer zero percent financing on occasion. While the term may be short, it is a great way to get a car without the burden of paying interest on it.

New cars are bought exclusively through new car dealerships, direct from the factory, or sometimes though membership organizations. New car dealerships are common and have a large selection of vehicles on site for you to look at and test drive. They also can bring in vehicles from other locations, including out of state, so you don't have to travel far to get the car you want. There are also factory direct vehicles such as Tesla. Tesla has a few small showrooms around, but you can't just show up and take a car home with you. It requires you to order your vehicle and then wait for it to be built. Lastly, some membership clubs like Sam's Club and Costco have the ability for their members to purchase vehicles. These are often at a slight discount compared to dealership vehicles, with the disadvantage being that you can't really test drive them ahead of time and they don't have their own maintenance

---

[40] Except the cars that are considered as antiques or collectibles. However, these cars are not driven as much.

departments.

Used cars have several advantages as well. Used vehicles are cheaper.[41] They can still be under warranty, or the dealership may offer a special extended warranty option on it. The rise in technology has also taken a lot of risk out of purchasing a used vehicle. Carfax reports can tell you whether the vehicle has ever been in a reported accident. It can also let you know the number of owners the vehicle has had. Dealerships will gladly provide these reports, or you can purchase one yourself if you are checking up on a car offered by an individual. Furthermore, if all the maintenance has been performed on a car at a dealership, it is easy to obtain a copy of the maintenance logs because they are electronic now.

While financing new cars is very cheap, dealerships still can facilitate great financing deals on used vehicles. I bought an eight-year-old Nissan Xterra when I finally needed a vehicle for myself. The dealership managed to arrange financing at 3.9 percent, which was better than the interest rate on my house at the time.[42]

If you are committed to getting a used vehicle, you can purchase it from a large dealership (think Toyota, Ford, Chevrolet, etc.), a small used car dealership, or from an individual seller. Be aware that car salesmen are paid by commission, and they can get very aggressive about selling you a vehicle. If you don't like that sort of confrontation, then you may want to look at buying from an individual seller.

Buying from individuals can take more time, as you have to sort through a lot of listings in different places and may struggle to find the exact car you want, but you may be able to get a much better deal. When buying from an individual, you should probably get a mechanic you trust to take a look at the car and see whether they can spot any issues that the seller isn't telling you about or doesn't know about. An individual is unlikely to give you a loan for the car, so you will need to work with a bank, credit union, or online lender for financing.

Ultimately, the choice of whether to buy a new or a used vehicle is up to

---

[41] There were periods when used vehicles were more expensive than new vehicles, but this is extremely rare. It was a combination of economic factors, including a government incentive for dealerships to scrap old cars that were traded in rather than to resell them. It dried up the availability of used cars and made some types of cars cheaper to buy new.

[42] Typically, interest rates on homes are lower than those on auto financing.

you and depends on your personality. Historically, I have bought used vehicles with low mileage and a single prior owner and have had good luck.

Auto Financing

A lot of dealerships offer financing on new and used vehicles. They partner with several different banks and lenders to get people financing. This type of financing is driven almost exclusively by your credit score and then can be influenced by the amount of cash you are putting as a down payment. If you have a poor credit score, you may experience a bait-and-switch moment. The dealer offers you financing and sends you home with the car only to call you back a few days later and demand a larger down payment because no one is willing to finance you and they need a larger down payment to get someone to take your loan.

If you are buying a car from an individual or a small dealership that doesn't have financing partners, then you can get an auto loan directly through your bank or credit union. When getting a loan directly from a bank, they may want more information than just your credit score. The banks I worked for wanted to verify your income by seeing your recent paystubs to determine whether you could afford payments on the vehicle. These banks did not partner with dealerships for financing, so they were not always comfortable with making loans for vehicle purchases.

Banks and credit unions are all different and have different standards. Some of them love financing vehicles; others hate it. As a result, they each have different standards for what they will accept. Often, lenders will not finance vehicles over ten years old. Vehicles this old have very little value, and banks do not want to deal with them if they have to take them back. I have also seen banks refuse to make auto loans of less than $5,000. If you are purchasing a car and need a loan less than this, they will make you an unsecured personal loan (assuming you have decent credit) and have it be repaid in two years or less. This may put a burden on your ability to repay. Lastly, I have also seen banks refuse to make loans less than a certain amount. One bank I worked for didn't make loans for less than $1,000; another wouldn't touch anything less than $2,500. By the time a bank goes through all the effort of putting together a loan, small loans like these end up costing more in labor and servicing[43] than they make in interest and fees.

---

[43] Servicing is the ongoing expense of collecting payments each month. It also

On average, people trade in their vehicle every three-five years to get a new(er) one. As a rule of thumb, you should avoid financing a vehicle for longer than five years and should try to make a three-year loan fit your budget. A three-year loan will allow you to build equity in the vehicle faster than it depreciates so you have something that is still valuable when you decide to turn it in.

Conversely, if you end up holding onto the vehicle for ten years, you will have seven years with no loan payment. You could save up for and pay cash for your next vehicle. A common savings trick is to continue to make the same payment you were making on the car but instead pay it into a savings account. If you have other debt, such as credit cards or student loans, you may wish to attack this debt with the freed-up payment amount instead each month.

Avoid long-term financing like the plague. Seven-year financing has become very common on new vehicles, and I have seen ten-year financing on expensive trucks and luxury cars. With such long-term financing, you are unlikely to build any equity into the vehicle as you own it, meaning you probably won't get any cash back out of it when you sell it. If you sell it midway through the financing term, you are likely just to get enough to pay off the financing (or you may have to cough up more money to finish paying off the loan). If you sell it at the end of ten years, the car will not be worth very much. A lot of pets don't even live for ten years, are you sure you want to commit to making a loan payment for that long?

---

includes the costs of collecting on a loan or repossessing a vehicle when payments are not being made.

Car Maintenance

Getting your oil changed every few months can be annoying. Getting the recommended maintenance done as it comes up can seem expensive. What's worse is if you don't do it.

Doing the recommended maintenance can save you from more costly repairs later and prevents an unhappy road-side breakdown. If you purchase a new car, a lot of this maintenance will be covered by warranty the first few years. Getting a used car may mean you are on the hook for paying for maintenance.

I prefer to take my cars to the dealership for maintenance because my feeling is that they know what to look for in their own cars better than independent shops. However, a lot of times I find it cheaper to get a recommendation from the dealership and then take it to an independent shop to get a large item fixed. The clutch was going out in our Scion Xb, and the dealer quoted us repair costs of $1,800. We took it to a local shop, and they fixed it for $700. It was a big savings for just a little bit of leg work. Another time they were the same price to get something repaired on a different car.

If you know a lot about cars, then feel free to do work yourself. Like home repairs (see chapter 14), doing your own car maintenance can save you a lot of money. I can swap out a battery by myself and save 40 percent of the cost that a dealership would charge me. I've also replaced small things like door handles and mirrors by following YouTube videos. I had a rear door hatch handle replaced at a local shop for $180 only to have the handle break again a few years later (a design flaw). I found the part for $40 and replaced it myself. Painting it may have cost more, but I left it black because I was more concerned about it functioning than the color. I also figured it would break again in a few years.

If you get nothing else from this chapter, I hope you take away how important it is to keep up on your car maintenance. This is because repairing an engine is much more costly than getting your oil changed a few times a year.

Auto Alternatives

I touched on this at the beginning of the chapter, but I think it is important to consider all the alternatives to owning a vehicle.

- WALK OR RIDE A BIKE – In addition to being the absolute cheapest, it will also help you stay fit and healthy. If you are serious about this alternative, consider getting a quality bicycle (not one you can get for $100 at a big box store). Good bikes can start as low as $500 and are much easier to ride. I was riding a cheap $100 bike at first until an old fat guy passed me like I was standing still. My commute took about forty minutes. I upgraded my bike, and my commute dropped to twenty-five minutes, and the old fat guy never passed me again.
- BUSES AND TRAINS – annual passes are very inexpensive, especially for students. If you need to ride in only bad weather, it may make more sense to just buy day passes occasionally and walk/bike the rest of the time. Check your math to see whether you should invest in an annual pass or note.
- UBER/LYFT – If your car payment is $300/mo, your insurance is $100/mo plus gas of $150/mo and maintenance that averages to $50/mo, you can afford up to $600 in rides before it makes more sense to get your own car. If the average ride costs $15 (typical for my area at the time of this writing), you can get forty rides a month. If there are twenty workdays in a month, that is a ride back and forth to work each day.
- SCOOTER AND BIKE RENTALS – In urban areas, scooter and bike rentals have become common. They allow you to get around more quickly (than walking) and not have the hassle of owning and storing a bike or a scooter.
- CARPOOLING OR RIDESHARING – Finding someone to carpool with is a great way to minimize your environmental impact and keep your costs down. Help them with gas occasionally, and everyone wins.
- TELECOMMUTE – Does your employer offer the option to work from home either full or part time? If they do, you can set up a small workspace in your home so you can skip the physical commute altogether.
- MOVE – If you live a long way from your place of employment, does it make sense to move closer? You can save time on your commute and at least reduce the use of your vehicle if not switch to one of the other alternatives completely. When we bought our first house, my wife and I deliberately picked a location that would allow us to walk to school and for her to walk to work.

Why I Want My Daughter to Know This

Owning a vehicle feeds into American consumerism. Having a car, especially a nice one, is a status symbol. However, you may not need a car at all with your lifestyle. If you can avoid car payments, auto insurance, gas, and maintenance you can easily save $600 per month per vehicle. That is a relatively inexpensive car as well.

If you do need a car, you should understand your options. My wife and I bought our first car together after we'd bought our first home. We looked around for quite a while. Every time our previous car was in the shop, we would look to see what cars we liked. We weren't well educated about car buying back then. We knew we wanted something economical that got good gas mileage.

When we finally did purchase a car, we were so excited that we didn't read all the fine print. After a lot of pressure, we agreed to a purchase price of $12,000. We signed the paperwork, and a few weeks later we received our first statement in the mail. We were on the hook for over $14,000—significantly more than we agreed to.

We started digging through our paperwork. Just less than $1,000 was for sales taxes and titling costs. We just hadn't thought about it, but those costs made sense. Over $1,000 ended up being for dealer handling and other vague fees that the dealership hadn't been forthright with us about.

In addition to everything else in this chapter, beware of shifty car dealers. They know more about the process than you. Your protection is that they must put it in writing. So don't sign anything unless you understand it. Pay attention to what costs they are really charging you.

11: MONEY AND RELATIONSHIPS

"Do you and Mom keep your money together?"

"Yes, we do. But many couples choose to keep the money they earn separately and to each contribute to shared expenses."

"How do you decide?"

"That's up to each couple and what they are comfortable with. It's a conversation you should have definitely before getting married but probably even before making any big purchases together like buying a car or renting an apartment."

"Why do you share money?"

"When Mom and I got married, we had nothing. Everything we've built, we've built together. Back then, it was easier to see whether we had enough money for bills when it was all together. Also, at various times, one of us has made significantly more than the other, while the other contributed to the family in other ways."

"How's that?"

"Well, when you were first born, Mom made more money and had health insurance through her work. She devoted everything to keeping that job and excelling at it, because we were in the middle of a really bad recession. I worked part time at a job that didn't pay as much. Instead, I was responsible for looking after you and doing a lot of things around the house. This was also when we bought a few of our rental properties, so I did all the repairs on them to get them ready to rent."

"Why would you not want to share money?"

"Well, if you work really hard, earn a lot of money, and decide to marry someone that earns less, you may not feel it is fair to share all your money with them—especially if they are bad at managing money. It doesn't mean you love them any less; you just have to make sure you have enough money to pay your bills."

I'm not going to tell you whether you should or shouldn't combine your finances with a significant other. That is a deeply personal question. I just want to show you what both options look like and make you aware of some things to be cautious about.

Combining Finances

Some of the biggest perks of combining finances is that it is very easy to manage. All the money goes into one account, and all bills get paid out of that account. Typically, this also means that you are both on the title of (own) any vehicles you have together and the apartment you rent or the home you own is in both your names. This makes it very easy to talk to banks about your accounts and your loans that you have together.

In this structure, often one of the partners will take the lead on managing the finances and provide direction to the other (preferably without fighting about it). When my wife and I first got married, I was in the Navy, and Rebecca wanted to manage the finances because she had the time and I didn't. I had managed my own finances up until then, but it bugged her that I had never balanced my checkbook.

After I had been discharged from the Navy after only a few months, we came back to Colorado and settled into a tiny one-bedroom house in November. We were extremely proud of that tiny little house, and I was content to let Rebecca continue to manage the finances.

It was bitter cold that winter, and the tiny house was old with no insulation. It didn't even have drywall, only thin paneling. Rebecca soon found two part-time jobs, but it took me a while longer. We both donated plasma, because together we could earn almost $300 a month. We were very concerned about money at this time, because we didn't have a lot coming in. To stay occupied around job hunting, we volunteered at the food bank. We had no TV, and the only radio was in the car. I had an old laptop, and we owned three movies that we rotated through. While we were volunteering at the food bank, they told us we should apply for assistance. We had some savings and some money coming in, and we were naïve and proud. We figured others needed it more, and we weren't that bad off.

After Rebecca started working some more, I was left at home many times with the thermostat not turned above 62 degrees. At night, we turned it down to 50 degrees. Because of the poor insulation, we would wake up and see frost on the ceiling and walls near our bed from our breath.

I froze and became grumpy. Rebecca froze at night only and then could go warm up at work for a while.

Finally, I broke down and sought heat assistance through our local utility company. I began filling out the paperwork and asked Rebecca for our financial information. As I filled out the paperwork, I noticed that over just two months of Rebecca's working and our donating plasma, we had saved an additional $200 while we froze to death and ate only top ramen.[44]

A big fight ensued because I was freezing and Rebecca refused to turn up the heat. When the heating assistance finally came through, I made a show of strutting over to the thermometer and dramatically turning it up to 68 degrees (and Rebecca still thought we should keep it down). Still, we turned it down to 60 degrees that night. It was one of the best night's sleep of my life.

After that, I took over handling the finances. I didn't want to freeze to death. I am pretty frugal but not nearly as tightfisted as my wife.

When you combine your finances, one of the biggest negatives is that one spouse is likely to be more of a spendthrift than the other. If the two of you can't come to an understanding, this will continue to cause problems in your relationship.

This can be exacerbated when one person makes significantly more than the other. That person may feel they are entitled to spend the money they've earned. Or they may feel that their partner shouldn't be able to spend their money so freely when they didn't earn it.

Separate Finances

My favorite structure I've seen for split finances is when each person keeps their own account, and they each pay a pre-determined amount into a joint account by a specified time each month. Then the joint bills, such as housing, are drafted from that account.

In their personal accounts, each person is responsible for paying their own bills, such as individual auto loans, insurance, student loans, etc. Then, if that person has money left over at the end of the month, they can spend or save it as they see fit.

Another structure is not to have any joint account, with each person paying their half (or other agreed-upon portion) directly to the bank/landlord/etc. However, if one person forgets to pay one month, the

---

[44] Not kidding. At this point in our lives, we would splurge once or twice a week and make a tuna helper (like a hamburger helper, but tuna was cheaper). On days we donated plasma, we would have cereal for breakfast. All other meals were ramen.

other person doesn't know about it until they get an angry phone call or letter demanding the rest of the payment.

Relationships and Taxes

When I was working as a tax preparer, my boss took extreme pleasure in marrying people. Filing a joint tax return with your boyfriend/girlfriend immediately qualifies you as common-law married in the eyes of the government.

My boss thought this was great and enjoyed making a big show about people getting hitched at the tax office. She was very energetic and positive about it, and the people that were getting married seemed to enjoy the enthusiasm.

A lot of these people were getting married because they got more money back on their tax returns. By filing together as "Married Filing Jointly," they were proclaiming to the government that they viewed themselves as, and wanted to be treated as, a married couple.

I usually cautioned people away from getting married at the tax office. At first, I thought it was cool, but then I realized that getting married for money was probably not the right reason. Especially when that money usually didn't add up to more than a couple of thousand dollars.

One of the first people that I discussed it with had been with her boyfriend for over twelve years and had three kids with him. They lived together and had a life together. When we talked about their being married, she recoiled, looked me in the eye, and said, "I don't love him that much. I don't want to have to get a divorce to leave him."

That sums up a big problem with filing a joint return when you are just dating someone. You've told the government you are married, and now you have to go through the government to get away from that person.

There are much more symbolic ways to get married, and I don't mean having an extravagant ceremony. My wife and I got married at a courthouse with only a judge and a bailiff present. My wife had a nice dress, and we had to pay the court costs. We spent less than $200 on the whole thing, and I remember every detail to this day. We've been together for 17 years so far.

You should spend a lot more time deciding on a spouse than in the space of a tax appointment. This is a major life decision. I won't get into details of all the things you should consider here, but I would just caution you NOT to get married by filing a joint tax return.

Once you are married, there are two ways to file your tax returns: Married Filing Jointly or Married Filing Separately. They are fairly self-explanatory. There are differences in their effects on each partner.

My experience has been that most married couples file a joint return. It is much simpler. It also may allow you to qualify for additional tax credits or higher tax credits. The big advantage is that joint filers have higher income thresholds for some taxes and deductions. This allows the couple to earn a larger amount of income before being pushed up into higher tax brackets.

It may make sense to file separate returns though if one spouse has significant medical bills or other expense that can be itemized that would allow them to complete Schedule A. This may be a lower threshold to reach with the income split up. However, if your spouse itemizes deductions, you are also required to itemize deductions.

Another reason to file separate returns would be if you intended to keep all your money separate. This doesn't help your tax situation but could prevent a spendthrift spouse from getting access to a large tax refund deposited into a joint account and spending it all. It can also provide peace of mind.

If you are out to maximize your tax refund (or minimize the amount you owe), you can prepare your taxes both ways and determine which way will benefit you the most. Then you file your tax return(s) whichever way benefits you the most. You can also change the way you file from year to year.

For more information about taxes and the documents mentioned in this section please refer to chapter 8.

Buying Stuff Together

Houses, cars, and pets are three common things you specifically need to think about when buying stuff with your significant other. A home is a big purchase and usually means a long-term commitment to a location and the person you are buying it with. Likewise, a car is another big purchase and may tie you to payments and a co-borrower for several years.

If you have any doubts about the person you are with, you may want to hold off on making a big purchase. Or make sure you can afford the payments without them. You can refer to chapter 14 for more information on buying a home, but ideally home payments shouldn't exceed 30 percent of your gross income, and many experts recommend keeping this to 25 percent.

Car expenses, including payments, insurance, gas, and maintenance, shouldn't exceed 10 percent of your gross income (see chapter 10 on a buying a car).

In the worst case scenario when your significant other leaves you with the house and at least one car payment, can you afford to make those payments on your own?

Another consideration is getting loans together. Homes and cars are often bought using loans. Sometimes, if one partner has bad credit, the banks will try to qualify the loan just based on the other partner. If this is a car, it may just be a credit check. If it is a home, they are looking at only one person's credit, income, and debt payments. As a rule, I believe that if you are the only one on the loan, you should be the only one on the title (only owner). In the event of a breakup or divorce, those items that you are responsible for are more likely to remain yours.

This doesn't mean that the partner doesn't get to use those things. In the event of a house, the partner would obviously live there with you. If it's a car, it may be a car for your partner to drive around. However, if you are the one legally responsible for making the loan payments, you should definitely be on the title and preferably the only one on the title. I have known instances when one person got the loan and another person took ownership. A few months later they broke up, and it got really messy.

You can also accumulate other debt together. The most common is credit cards. They are easy to get, and you can be joint owners. Again, if one partner is irresponsible with their spending, they can rack up credit card debt that you both are on the hook for paying back. Another option is for you to get a credit card and then add your significant other as an authorized user. In the event your significant other handles the card poorly or you separate, you can easily close their card.

Be wary of getting any type of loan together if you are not fully committed to your partner. This is especially true if you have more money, earn more money, or have better credit. Banks don't care which partner pays them back if they are both on the loan. However, in the event of default, they will concentrate their collection efforts on the partner that has a better ability to repay the loan.

Lastly, I think it is important to consider the financial impact of getting pets together. Some pets are inexpensive to obtain and inexpensive to maintain. However, they are a long-term commitment together. If you get an expensive pet that requires special food and regular veterinary bills, it could be costly in the event you part ways with your significant other. A pet may also increase the amount of rent you have to pay (see chapter 13).

When you adopt a pet, you are agreeing to take care of it for years. During the Great Recession,[45] I saw people turn their pets back into animal shelters because they could no longer afford to keep them. Worse, some people just took the collars off and turned their pets loose in unfamiliar neighborhoods. Don't be like that. Know that a pet is a long-term financial commitment.

Preparing for Divorce, Disability, and Death

I'm lucky in that I haven't had to deal with any of these myself. I did watch my parents go through a divorce when I was twenty, and I often worked with people trying to sort out their finances during and after a divorce and after the loss of a loved one.

I hope that you and your significant other live a long happy life together and that by the time you die it's your kids' or grandkids' responsibility to sort out your money.

There are several events that could negatively impact your finances throughout your life. The one that leaves people with a lot of resentment is divorce (or a break-up if you are not married to the person). When two people decide to part ways, they often have stuff together. Things that they could afford together, they can no longer afford on their own. This is why a lot of times during a divorce, they are forced to sell their home.

Sometimes during a divorce, loans that both people signed on go unpaid either purposefully or through neglect. Either way, this hurts your credit at a time when you are trying to find a new place to live. A lot of these negatives keep adding up and are one of the main reasons why divorce is so devastating financially.

The other main reason is that your significant other walks away with half the equity[46] that you've built together. A couple that has accumulated a

---

[45] The Great Recession was a period from the end of 2007 through most of 2009 that saw many people lose their homes and jobs more than at any other time in recent history. It took several years for most people and the country to recover from the financial problems that started during this time.

[46] Equity in a home (or possibly in a vehicle or other asset) is the difference between what it is worth and what you owe on it. If you own a $500,000 home with no loan, then you have $500,000 worth of equity. If you owe $300,000 on that home, then you have only $200,000 of equity.

million dollar net worth suddenly each finds themselves a long way away from being millionaires after a divorce.

A lot of states assume that all assets in a marriage are owned equally. This becomes devastating to one person that may have built up a million dollars and then marries a deadbeat that walks away with $500,000 of their money after a few years.

If you are concerned about this happening to you, the best way to prevent it is through a prenuptial agreement (sometimes referred to as a "prenup"). A good prenup should spell out what happens to your finances in the event of a divorce, separation, or even death of one person. Prenups are prepared before you get married by an attorney.

Prenups are a difficult subject to broach with your partner. At a time when you both love each other so much that you want to announce it to the world, it seems ridiculous to consider the possibility that your marriage may end in a divorce.

As they say, the number one leading cause of divorce is marriage![47]

There is a way to open up a conversation about a prenup, without immediately talking about a divorce. If you approach your partner about a prenup and the way it will affect each of your families in the event one of you dies, you are more likely to get them to buy into it. It is still not likely to be a fun conversation.

Once your partner is open to the subject, you can get a lawyer involved to help draft a prenup. The lawyer can help guide you both through the unpleasantness of discussing a divorce.

Of course, death is another big event that can negatively impact your finances. In addition to being emotionally devastated, you suddenly are faced with the loss of your partner's income. Just like with a divorce, dealing with the death of a significant other may force you to sell your home and move somewhere cheaper. The best way to protect against this is to each have life insurance. In the event of a death, the beneficiary[48] (typically the surviving spouse) receives cash to use how they see fit (see chapter 15 for more information on types of life insurance and guidance on choosing how much you should get).

The surviving spouse can struggle further if the one that died was the one

---

[47] The actual leading cause of divorce is basic incompatibility, followed by infidelity, and then money, https://institutedfa.com/Leading-Causes-Divorce/.
[48] Beneficiary is the person that would receive the life insurance funds.

that handled all the finances. Often, the surviving spouse doesn't know where bank accounts are, how much are in them, what loans they must make payments on, whether there is life insurance, or other types of accounts.

Regardless of who handles the money, it is a good idea to keep a list of accounts somewhere and do your best to keep it updated.[49] That way, if one of you should pass away, the surviving spouse has resources to track down where money is at as well as where the will and any life insurance policies are.

A lawyer is a good resource for preparing for death. They can guide you through the process of each creating a will, power of attorney, end-of-life instructions, and more. In the past, my wife and I have both had holographic wills. Not as cool as they sound, a holographic will is just handwritten and signed by the person creating it. Ours were rudimentary and didn't survive much beyond buying our first home and our daughter being born.

We then used a will-maker computer program. It cost less than $100 and helped guide us through a lot more options than we realized were available. As of this writing, we are now in talks with a lawyer to prepare wills and trusts for each of us. We are playing catch-up on this, as it is recommended to have a good will established once you have kids or accumulate anything of significant value.

Lastly, it is important to be aware of your options in the event of a disability or serious illness. This may be a disability or illness that occurs to you, your spouse, your kids, or a loved one that you end up taking care of. There is no way to ever get truly prepared for such an eventuality, but there are some things you can do to mitigate the risk and some social safety nets in place you should be aware of.

By focusing on maintaining good health (see chapter 12), you greatly reduce the possibility of a lot of illnesses. You can also purchase disability or accident insurance.[50] Some employers will provide accident or disability insurance to protect their employees from a sudden loss of income. Check with your employer to see whether you are already covered.

There are also social programs that act as a safety net. I can't begin to tell you about all of them because I don't know about all of them. I can tell you

---

[49] As I wrote this, I realized I haven't been taking my own advice and need to write a list of accounts. I do have a list of passwords that Rebecca will need. I also have a list of the properties we own together and what entities they are in.
[50] Aflac is the provider I have heard of most often. I also listened to their pitch repeatedly at various jobs I worked at.

that Supplemental Security Income (SSI) is a program that the government has to help provide income for people with disabilities. There are countless local organizations, such as places of worship and food banks, which can get you plugged into other programs that will help you continue to survive in the event of a disability. Additionally, many corporations do have hearts after all. Many banks have programs to defer mortgage payments for a few months until a person can get back on their feet. Many for-profit hospitals have financial aid packages you can apply for to either reduce or pay for your out-of-pocket medical expenses.

Be aware of the *Family and Medical Leave Act* (FMLA). This law requires employers to allow their qualified employees[51] to take time off to deal with serious health conditions for themselves or certain relatives. It also allows them to take time off for the birth or adoption of a child. The employer is required to allow the employee to come back to work in the same or similar position. During the leave, the employee's health insurance must be maintained with the employee continuing to maintain their portion of out-of-pocket costs.

When Should You Talk about Money in a Relationship?

Early and Often.

It's not a first-date conversation. Probably not even a second- or third-date conversation. About the time you begin to think about what your life would be like together in the future is when you should talk about money with your potential partner.

You want to make sure you are money compatible. Compatible doesn't mean you both need to have the same money-management style. *Compatible* means that your potentially different styles should work well together. You are already making sure you are compatible in other ways, so making sure you are money compatible isn't a stretch. You should find out about the other person's credit. Do they like to borrow money to make purchases? Do they carry high credit card balances? Are they a spender or a saver?

Once you've felt each other out, you will need to come up with a plan for how you are going to manage your money together moving forward. Are you going to keep separate accounts or a joint account? This should likely be

---

[51] See whether you and your company qualify, https://www.dol.gov/agencies/whd/fmla.

decided around the time you move in together or decide you are getting serious.

Just moving in together can easily be handled with separate accounts and likely will be for a while. As you two come closer together, it becomes natural to handle more and more money together.

If you are already in a committed relationship and haven't talked about money yet, you need to do it immediately. You need to make sure you are both pulling in the same direction when it comes to money. If you never talk about money, it can obstruct the intimacy between you. It could be because resentments build from perceived mismanagement. Or because you never disclose and discuss a side of you both that is very personal.

You should get to a point with your significant other that you feel comfortable talking about money as often as needed. My wife and I discuss money topics at least once a week outside of our discussions about handling business affairs and money. It is never an open-and-shut conversation either. We continually discuss whatever money topics we are working on.

I left my job in August 2019 prematurely to pursue my own business. I had been unhappy for months. Leading up to the decision, my wife and I discussed what our financial situation would look like. We had hoped that the business would be open and generating revenue by December of that year. Instead, it took almost five extra months. We had planned for that possibility together though.

When the time came that I couldn't stand it anymore, I called up my wife and said I needed to quit right then. She said okay, because we knew we had the reserves to last us for a while and she was still working. We didn't need to discuss it further.

Following my departure from that job, we continued to discuss whether (1) I should get a part-time job until the business opened, and (2) we needed to cut back on expenses and which ones.

I said earlier in this chapter that I manage the finances for our house, but I don't do it alone. Every decision I've made was based on continual discussions with my wife. She doesn't pay the bills, doesn't know what bank our mortgage is through, and doesn't even know how much she makes at her job because it doesn't matter to her.

She does know that our main financial goals are to build a successful business, maximize our retirement savings, help our daughter through college, and have money for travelling. She also knows that to reach these goals we may make small sacrifices like not ordering sodas when we go out to eat, driving older vehicles, or avoiding cable bills (see chapter 21 for all the ways we actually cut expenses).

Our money philosophy is the same. We decided on it together, and we continue to refine it together.

Why I Want My Daughter to Know This

Actively talking about money with your partner helps manage expectations for both of you. How you manage your finances together shouldn't be an accident. You need to have a good understanding of how your significant other manages money, how you manage money, and then develop a plan on how you will manage your money together.

I started writing this chapter at the end of December 2019. In January 2020, Rebecca's sister was diagnosed with brain cancer at the age of 38. It became a struggle to finish this chapter, as many of the concepts hit close to home.

Many of the concerns that we had for her sister, her husband, and her kids revolved around money. How much were cancer treatments going to cost? Could they survive a short-term loss of her income? What if the worst should happen, would her husband be able to financially maintain the household and raise the kids?

The good thing was that she had done some planning ahead of time. She had an emergency fund, which she could draw on. Her work did have employer-paid insurance with a maximum out-of-pocket, which drastically capped how much she would spend annually on doctor's visits.

But there were things they could have done to be more prepared.

This struggle helped my wife and I become more thoughtful in planning for our own final chapter. We want to make sure our daughter is well provided for. We want to make sure that if something happened to one of us, the other wouldn't lose everything.

As unpleasant as it is to talk about death, it is better and easier to discuss it ahead of time. You will get emotional about it. But not nearly as emotional as you would get if you had the conversation when your partner was actually dying.

12: YOUR HEALTH

My daughter ended up getting two staples in the back of her head right before
Christmas one year.

"When are we going to get the staples out, Dad?"

"It's almost healed. It looks good," I replied. "I think we could get them out next
week."

"Do we have to go back to the emergency room?"

"Well, I googled it and was thinking we can get them out ourselves."

"What?" she asked in horror.

"Yeah, it's simple. I can show you videos on YouTube. They cut the staple in half with
a pair of wire cutters and then you can pull them right out."

"Doesn't a doctor need to do it?"

"Why?" I asked.

"Because they're doctors and that's what they do."

"It's not that hard. Just watch the videos. It's simple. Besides, your Mom really wants
to do it."

"It's going to hurt," she objected.

"Not any more than if a doctor did it. Besides, we can ice it first to numb the area."

She swallowed hard. Still nervous.

"Let's watch the video together so you can see how easy it is."

This chapter isn't here to tell you what to eat or how much you should work
out. Other books by experts in nutrition and exercise science are devoted to
those things. This chapter is to show you why those things are important.

In my early twenties, we were broke and living on cheap food. Cheap
food is not always very healthy food. We did it out of necessity, but it also
instilled some bad habits in me. I needed years to break out of them.

In addition to not eating well, I wasn't exercising. I worked at an ice
cream store that required me to be on my feet for six–eight hours a day.

Going for a run after a hard shift on my feet didn't sound appealing at all.

I got fat.

I got up to 250 pounds of unhealthy weight, and I carried that weight around for about seven years. These were some of the worst years of my life for my health. I was constantly sick. I had stomach issues the entire time, unrelenting heartburn, and I caught every virus that came through town.

I didn't know I was unhealthy. I just assumed everyone got sick like this. My wife didn't get as sick, but she was always healthier than me, so I didn't think much about it. It was the time when she also carried around some extra weight, so she was also sick a lot. Her solution was to ignore it. Mine was to wallow in misery.

There was no single pivotal moment for me when I decided to get in shape. It was the sum of small decisions.

My wife and I signed up for Zumba and loved it, so we consistently did it for a couple of years. That helped me lose a few pounds. But I was still working at an ice cream shop and eating junk, so a lot of the weight stayed.

Then I got a job at a bank. The bank had cookies and seemed to have free food around every other week, but my level of junk food fell off drastically. Just switching jobs allowed me to lose another 15 pounds of weight.

My wife and I shared one car, and it got a little cumbersome for her to drop me off before heading to work. So I began biking to work.

At about the same time, mud runs and obstacle course races boomed, and we fell in love with them. We stopped doing Zumba but began running at least one race every weekend during the warm months. I was motivated to do my best so I downloaded a Couch to 5K app and began training three times a week.

The running helped with part of the races, but obstacles were hard because I didn't have much strength. So my wife and I joined a CrossFit® gym with unlimited classes each week. If you haven't noticed by now, I am kind of cheap and so is my wife. To make the most of our unlimited class investment, we attended classes at least five times a week.

At my most active, I was running for thirty minutes three times a week, doing CrossFit five times a week, biking to work three–four times a week, and running a race every weekend.

I ate whatever I wanted and got down to 185 pounds, with a total loss of 65 pounds.

However, it wasn't sustainable for a number of reasons. I ended up buying a car and switching jobs. Biking fell off quickly. CrossFit fell off when we decided to focus on other financial priorities. Races became more scarce as companies went out of business. The new job wouldn't allow me to run on my lunch break, and some other issues, like plantar fasciitis in my feet, interfered as well.

I still worked out, but some of the weight came back. Focusing on nutrition became as important as exercising. Plantar fasciitis made it painful to run for nearly a year until I got it completely rehabbed. Nutrition also became an important way to make sure I was getting the proper nutrients to prevent an injury.

Even though some of the weight has come back, I have not been as sick as before—when I was 250 pounds. I rarely get colds, most of my stomach issues have resolved themselves, I sleep better, and my mood has improved a lot.

Staying healthier helps me save money and make money. I no longer spend as much money at the doctor's office as I used to, because I don't need to go as often. I also spend less on medication (such as antacids and cold medicine).

Staying healthy helps me make money, because I haven't had to take sick days from work as much. When I was working hourly part time, taking a day off for illness meant losing out on the income earned that day. When I moved to full time, not using sick days meant I could use the time off for vacations or other fun things.

Make use of your health insurance and go to the doctor when you need to. Many health insurance programs allow you to go in for an annual check-up without having so much as a co-pay. It's a good idea to chat with a professional about what is going on with your body.

Our local grocery store offers a walk-in clinic if you have simple things like the flu or pink eye that you need a simple prescription for. The cost is minimal. When we didn't have insurance, this was the best bet for us. Check around for your own walk-in clinics.

There is usually one low-cost clinic in most communities that is structured to help people who are struggling financially. Ask around and see whether there is one near you. We never used ours, but we knew where it was in case we needed it.

In our twenties and early thirties, my wife and I were the worst about going to the doctor, primarily because we didn't want to pay for it. Sprain an ankle? Ice, elevate, and support! Deep cut? Superglue it shut! Shoot yourself with a nail gun? Slap a band-aid on it! Get killed? Walk it off!

This approach did lead us to suffer with some problems that were easily remedied. I suffered from plantar fasciitis for nearly a year, convinced I could solve it with advice from Google. I finally went to see a physical therapist, and 90 percent of my symptoms were gone in six weeks.

Don't sacrifice your health for money. It's not worth it.

Why I Want My Daughter to Know This

Fitness became such an important part of my life that I got my daughter involved in every physical activity that she wanted. Dance (hip-hop, ballet, and cheer), swimming, softball, volleyball, karate,[52] and gymnastics. Not all at the same time, but there was rarely a time when she wasn't doing at least one. These were on top of non-physical activities like choir and band.

Then we moved.

My daughter, who had been so outgoing and social, now felt isolated and depressed. She didn't want to do anything. She didn't want to participate in clubs, and she didn't want to do any sports.

In addition to being worried about our daughter's adjusting to her new school, we were now concerned for her health. We had gone through unhealthy times ourselves. We knew it was easier to maintain fitness than to rebuild it.

So, we walked the dog a lot more and made Ashla come with us. We rode bikes together a lot of places in our new town. When we did physical challenges,[53] we forced her to do a few of them with us.

I never want anyone, but especially Ashla, to be as unhealthy as I was. Quality of life is so much better when you devote time and money to maintaining your health.

---

[52] She eventually earned her Junior Black Belt.
[53] Such as thirty squats a day for thirty days. They are a good way to get back into working out or add something when your workouts start to lag.

13: RENTING YOUR FIRST PLACE

"Where do you go to rent an apartment? Is there like an apartment store?" Ashla asked me.

"No, not really."

"Well, I know you can't trust people on the Internet, so I wouldn't go meet someone off of Craigslist."

"That is where most people rent places right now," I stated. "Another place is Facebook Marketplace. Both are free. Neither existed when your Mom and I were looking for our first place. We found it by driving around and looking for "For Rent" signs and calling them. It was slow and took time. Now I would probably go to a property manager like the one we use to manage our rentals and see what they had in our price range."

"So... you would go to meet a stranger off the Internet at their house?"

Before you go out and start looking for an apartment or a house to rent, you should figure out what you can afford, where you're willing to live, and how big of a place you need. When I was in the Navy, we were assigned to base housing. My brand-new wife and I were assigned to a three-bedroom/two-bathroom house. At the time, everything we owned could fit in a VW Jetta with both of us in it.

We spent the first night sleeping on a leaky air mattress that we had to blow up twice in the middle of the night. We bought an inexpensive bed the next day. Rebecca's parents bought us a washer and dryer for a wedding gift, and we had that delivered the next week.

Other than that, we owned nothing. We slept in one bedroom, kept our clothes in another bedroom, and couldn't find a use for the third bedroom, so we just shut the door and pretended it didn't exist. We alternated showering in the two different bathrooms based on what we felt like that day. Our kitchen table consisted of the cardboard box that a vacuum cleaner we had bought came in.

If we'd been assigned a one-bedroom/one-bathroom apartment, we still wouldn't have had enough stuff to fill half of it. We weren't paying for it, so we thought it was great fun.

Several months later, when we were back in Colorado and looking for a place that we would be paying for, we were more focused on the price of rent than anything else. When we were looking for a place to rent, we didn't have a good idea of how much we could afford. Neither of us had jobs at the time. We were struggling to find work and were worried that employers weren't taking us seriously because we didn't have an address in the area.

With that in mind, Rebecca (who was still in charge of the finances at that time) found a place for $250 per month. It was a run-down motel, which had been converted to studio apartments. It was in one of the worst parts of town and sat right next to a convenience store on a busy street. All the windows had bars over them, and the whole place looked vacant. It had been vandalized in a number of places, and it looked like a stiff breeze might knock it over.

A one-bedroom apartment at that time ran for $600 a month, so this place was a steal. But I thought we might die if we lived there. The next place we found was a tiny one-bedroom house with the smallest bathroom you can imagine and a kitchen that couldn't hold more than one person at a time. The rent was $425 per month. Somehow, we convinced this guy to rent us the place, even though we didn't have jobs. We had the security deposit and the first month of rent. So, he let us move in.

While we lived there, our car was broken into one morning. Once, we had to call the cops on our neighbors because we thought there was serious domestic violence occurring (turned out they were brother and sister and just liked to fight—they both told us this). People were constantly wandering around the area drunk. A couple of nearby houses got vandalized. Three houses close by were rented by college students that partied every Wednesday, Friday, and Saturday.

And we still were grateful to have the place because it was way better than the $250 death motel.

How Much Can You Afford? Should You Get a Roommate?

As a landlord now, I know that the guy we first rented from shouldn't have rented to us. We had no income. Typically, I like to see my tenants have three–four times the rent in income each month. On our rent of $425 per month, we should have had pay stubs from a job, showing our gross income was at least $1,275 to $1,700 per month. A three-time multiple of rent is common, but it is the absolute minimum most landlords will consider. A four-time multiple provides a greater level of confidence that the potential tenants will be able to afford the rent.

When you are young and single, it can make a lot of sense to get a roommate to better afford the rent on a place. Going from a one-bedroom to a two-bedroom apartment is not likely to double your rent. More commonly, the rent will increase from 30 to 50 percent. This means your overall rent is more; however, because you are sharing that cost, you each spend less.

For example, a one-bedroom apartment may cost you $750 a month, whereas a two-bedroom apartment may cost $1,000. By splitting this cost with another person, you are now paying only $500 a month. This is a great strategy to save money and possibly get a larger place in a better neighborhood.

I would encourage you to get a place that you can afford completely on your own. You should be able to pay the entire $1,000 a month in case your roommate can't pay or decides to move out. You don't want to end up getting evicted over it. Both of you will be signing the lease, and you both are responsible for the entire amount. The landlord will not care how you split it up. If your roommate can't pay one month, the landlord still expects the full amount.

You also need to make sure your roommate is someone you can get along with and is also financially responsible. You will both be signing on the lease. If your roommate doesn't pay their share of the rent, you are then responsible for it. Failing to pay for them could get you both evicted.[54] If they put utilities into their name and fail to pay, you may find yourself without power, water, or heat one day. Make sure you both have come to an agreement on how and by when you will be paying the landlord and for the utilities. A lot of working with a roommate is similar to handling finances with a significant other as was discussed in chapter 11.

Everyone thinks having their best friend as a roommate is a great idea. I did too when I came out of high school. During my freshman year of college,

---

[54] An eviction is when a landlord goes through the court and sheriff's office to sever your lease and physically remove you and your stuff from the property. This is something that future landlords can see when doing a background check on you. An eviction makes getting a future apartment much more difficult.

my best friend and I signed up to live together in the dorms. Everyone warned us not to do this, but we did it anyway. Within a couple of months, we hated each other so much that I had to request to be moved to another dorm. Living with each other ruined our friendship.

It ended up being much easier for me to be angry with and forgiving of a person I just met. With a friend I had known for four years, it was different. Both roommates irritated me in their own ways. But the one I had just met didn't come with any expectations. My friend, on the other hand, expected us to hang out all the time, while I expected that we would each do most things on our own.

Since college, my wife and I have had roommates move into our house at various times. All of them were friends, and we got along much better. For us, it worked better that we were the landlord and the friend paid us money for rent. For you, this may mean qualifying to rent a place on your own and putting everything in your name and then have someone rent an extra room from you. This way, you don't have to worry about someone else wrecking your credit. You also know that you can afford to pay for everything if your roommate doesn't pay.

Looking for a Place

Once you've determined how much you can afford and whether you are going to have roommates, you can begin to shop around for a place to live. As I said earlier, the most common places where I've seen rentals listed online is Craigslist and Facebook Marketplace, because they are free to post. A lot of small landlords use them to get their few rentals listed. However, many property management companies will also post some of their listings out there to capture leads on potential tenants.

Finding property management companies through Craigslist or Facebook Marketplace is a possibility, but you can also google property management companies in your area. Property managers are a good way to access more potential properties. They are likely to have an inventory of currently available places to rent and have an idea of what places will be coming up for rent soon. Property managers are likely to understand landlord and tenant laws a lot better than small landlords. This will help protect you and your rights.

In the days before the Internet, driving around was a good way to identify places to rent, and it still can be. You may drive past a large apartment building that you would like to live in. They may not have anything out on the

Internet at that time, but if you stop by, they are likely to have an on-site manager and a display unit that you can tour right then. They can then give you an idea of what they will have coming up for rent.

Driving around is also a way to identify other property management companies by their signs in yards or independent landlords that choose not to put their properties up on the Internet. Having lived in a college area, I can tell you that landlords needed only to put a sign in the yard every May to attract numerous college kids looking for a place to live the next academic year.

Looking at all of these options will help you identify average prices for properties as well as determine what amenities you have available to you. Large apartment complexes sometimes have pools, parks, dog runs, or are conveniently located near bus stops. Smaller places may lack amenities but make up for it with cheaper rents or proximity to areas of interest.

The Application and Hidden Expenses

Once you have identified a place you'd like to live, the landlord will require that you complete an application. An application gives the landlord basic information about you. Often, it also authorizes them to run either a background check, a credit check, or both. They likely will ask for references, which usually includes the name and phone number of your previous landlord if you've had one. Landlords can share only so much information legally, but they have gotten good at reading between the lines and can determine whether the previous landlord had a bad impression of you.

An application is your place to shine. I've seen numerous applications half complete. An unfinished application tells me the applicant doesn't really care whether they get to live in my place. It also tells me they are likely sloppy and will treat my rental with the same sloppiness.

Remember from chapter 1 that winners win. A complete application with good references is your chance to put your best foot forward and show the landlord that you are serious, neat, and take care of details. Comparing two otherwise identical applications to rent my place, I would pick the one that is most complete and legible. Many of the same principles from chapter 3 regarding filling out a job application can also be applied to filling out an application for an apartment.

Don't be surprised if the landlord charges an application fee. Application fees vary from $25 to $50, with the majority usually being at the high end of that range. This fee discourages people that aren't serious or don't have the financial means to really rent the place from applying. Don't think that the landlord is making money off this fee though. Application fees go to reimburse the landlord for the costs of running credit and background checks.

When the landlord does credit and background checks (if their state allows it), they will find out that you have a good credit and a clean record. If you've presented yourself as a great potential tenant, they will want you to move in as soon as possible. So you will need to have your security deposit and your first month's rent on hand.

A security deposit protects the landlord from any damage you may do to the apartment/home over and above normal wear and tear. If you live there for five years and move out upon the end of your lease, and the carpet is wearing thin and the walls need to be repainted, you should get the entire security deposit back because those items would need to be replaced and repainted regardless.

On the other hand, live there for three months and stop paying (requiring the landlord to evict you), leave a hole burned in the carpet and permanent marker drawings on the wall, and then the landlord will keep your security deposit to help offset the cost of added repairs and the court costs related to the eviction (see later in this chapter for more details on evictions).

If you've got pets, don't expect that the landlord will automatically allow them or that they will get to live there for free. Many landlords don't allow fish tanks over a certain size for fear of their place getting flooded. They may also exclude large dogs for fear of their attacking someone or because of the extra wear and tear they do to floors. Even if the landlord does allow pets, they may charge a higher security deposit or additional "pet rent."

Reading Your Lease

When you have been accepted by the landlord and are presented with the lease, your instinct may be to sign it as quickly as possible so they can't take it back. You should make a habit of reading your lease and ask the landlord about anything that doesn't seem right. If you aren't comfortable with the lease, ask to take it with you to have a friend, parent, or mentor review it with you. Beware of a landlord that pressures you to sign when you aren't comfortable.

Most leases are required to be written in plain language. This is good because you don't need to be a lawyer to understand what is in them. A lease will spell out a variety of terms. Below are some of the most common ones, regardless of what state you live in:

- Who the landlord is and the names of those renting from them.
- Address of the property you are renting.
- The length of lease term. Standard rental terms are for one year. Some landlords do shorter leases (especially in student housing). Sometimes a landlord allows a month-to-month lease, meaning you are not locked in for a long time. Most leases automatically convert to a month-to-month lease after their initial term expires.
- The amount of the monthly rent.
- The rent due date. Most of the time, this is the first of the month.
- What day the rent is considered late, and how much you will be charged for late fees. Pay on time and avoid unnecessary fees.
- Returned-check fees. If you bounce a check to the landlord, they are going to charge you for it. This may also make you late on your rent, and then you incur additional fees.
- The landlord's policy when accepting money when the rent is past due. Most landlords state in their leases that any money received is first applied to past-due rent before any amount is applied to current rent or fees. (Changes in tenant/landlord law may alter this.)
- The amount of the security deposit.
- The security deposit due time. When you move out, how long the landlord has to return it to you or inform you why it is not being returned.
- The utilities policy. Whether you or the landlord will be paying for the utilities.
- The existing damage policy. The landlord requires the tenant to provide a list of any damage upon moving in. This makes the damage the landlord's responsibility when you move out. You should keep a copy of this list and photos of the damage in case the landlord tries to blame you for the damage when you move out and wants to keep your security deposit to pay for it. This includes pest infestation.
- Who can use the property, or how many people can use the property. This is to control wear and tear of the unit as well as to limit undesirable people from living in the property who would not have made it past the landlord's background check.

- The pet deposit amount or pet fee as well as the additional rent per pet.

- The entry and inspection policy stating that the tenant shall allow the landlord and their agents to enter the property at any reasonable time to make repairs, show the property, or to inspect it. In Colorado, it is customary for a landlord to give tenants 24–48 hours' notice. In the event of an emergency, they may also enter at unreasonable times.

- Many landlords' non-smoking policy. In Colorado, this also prohibits marijuana (since it is legal in the state). Smoke is very difficult to clean out of places, and your violating this policy allows the landlord to keep your security deposit.

- The insurance policy explaining that the landlord's insurance covers damage to the building only, not your stuff. Some landlords may require that you get your own (renter's) insurance that covers the loss of your stuff. However, many landlords will leave it up to you to decide whether you want this insurance. (See chapter 15 for more information on insurance.)

- The lease stating that the landlord has no liability[55] to the tenant or a guest in the event there is an injury, damage, or loss.

- House Rules, Homeowner Associations (HOAs), Ordinances, and Statutes Policy explaining that both you as the tenant and the landlord agree to follow any laws and abide by any rules of the house (when you rent just a unit and several people share common areas) and any home-owner association's rules, including satisfactorily correcting any issues arising from Code Compliance.

- Roommate disputes not being the landlord's problem. The lease will spell out when a roommate is no longer liable for paying rent and when the landlord will release the security deposit.

- The repairs policy. It is important because it states that you agree that everything in the place currently works (unless noted in the damage list) and that you agree to give back the property in the same condition. It also states that any repairs or alterations to the property that the tenant wants to do need to be approved by the landlord first. It also states what repairs are the landlord's responsibility.

- The snow removal policy, which is important in colder climates. It may not even exist in some states. This policy specifies whether the

---

[55] Meaning they don't owe them anything.

landlord or the tenant is responsible for snow removal and when that needs to be completed by.

- The yard maintenance policy describing the tenant's or landlord's responsibility when it comes to the care of the yard.
- The default and substantial lease violations clauses stating that a violation of any part of the lease is cause for eviction. It is at the landlord's discretion whether they will allow the tenant to stay. Most of the time landlords will pursue an eviction only when the tenant stops paying rent. However, problem tenants are evicted for lesser things.
- The waiver clause stating that if the landlord fails to enforce any part of the lease it is not considered a waiver and that part (and the entire lease) are still enforceable. This also includes rent whereby a landlord is still entitled to the full amount, even if they accept a partial payment of rent.
- Contingency capping the amount of attorneys' fees that can be awarded to either the tenant or the landlord in the event one party prevails over the other if issues arise and attorneys are engaged. It will also state that any judgment shall be paid promptly.
- Lease transfer and full enforceability in the event the landlord changes (either through the sale of the property or just a change in the company that manages the property). This is typically called an assignment clause.
- Conditions under which the landlord will disclose information on the tenant and their rental history.
- Foreclosure[56] and the protection of the tenant from losing their home, with the lease remaining in effect.
- The process of moving out at the end of the lease and the steps required to be taken. This includes giving the landlord proper notice (typically thirty days) of their intent to move out (rather than continue paying month to month or renew for a longer term). It describes the condition the property must be in when returned to the landlord.

---

[56] Foreclosure is when the property owner (which is sometimes the landlord) fails to make payments and the bank takes the property.

What's an Eviction?

An eviction is when you get kicked out of the place. This happens when you either fail to pay the rent or violate some other term of the lease. After a few days, the landlord can serve you with a Right to Cure notice, which demands payment (or a correction of a different violation). If you don't abide, several days later the landlord engages the court to legally sever the lease and allow the landlord to kick you out. Following your court date, the landlord typically has to engage a police officer to come out the same day as a moving crew. Many states allow the landlord to move your stuff onto the curb, and it is up to you to collect it before it gets stolen or damaged by weather. After some time, the landlord has the right to haul it all to the dump. It is difficult to give an accurate timeline, because each state (and sometimes each county and city) has different rules to help protect tenants and give them time to pay rent and keep their home. Also, these rules can change with different laws coming into effect.

I Want My Security Deposit Back

If you terminate a lease early (especially if you are evicted) or fail to give proper notice that you are moving out, you may no longer be entitled to get your entire security deposit back. Most commonly, you can lose your security deposit for damage that is outside of normal wear and tear. As discussed previously, this includes smoking in the unit or pest control issues that you don't take care of. It is very important that you take care of the place if you want your money back.

Why I Want My Daughter to Know This

Writing this chapter was a struggle for me. I only ever signed one lease as a tenant. I got to know tenant/landlord law a lot better when I became the landlord. I've taken numerous classes on property management and keep up to date on changes in the law. I've personally reviewed dozens of leases with tenants and now look over the leases my property manager uses.

A young person signing a lease on their first or second place is at a disadvantage to knowing and understanding what is in the lease and what their rights under the law are. My feeling is that most of the laws are written to protect tenants, not landlords. However, most tenants don't know enough about those laws, and some landlords can be shady.

If my daughter ever runs into a shady landlord, she should know that the *Fair Housing Act* prohibits discrimination in home sales, financing, and rental, based on race, color, disability, familial status, religion, sex, or national origin. Here in Colorado, the state has taken it a step further and also prohibits discrimination based on ancestry, creed/belief system, marital status, or sexual orientation.[57]

---

[57] Colorado has a website to educate people about a variety of rental, fair housing, and home-owner issues, which is worth checking out, http://www.coloradohousingconnects.org/.

14: BUYING YOUR FIRST HOME

"This is the house you got me?" Ashla asked. She was six years old, and we had made the decision to purchase a rental property for her at that time for the sole purpose of paying for her college one day.

"That's right," I said. "We've got some work to do on it, and you are going to help us."

She ran around the house for a bit looking into all the rooms. It had a basement apartment that was already rented out. Ashla was concerned about it. "So, they are going to keep living here?" she asked.

"That's the idea. The rent they pay will help pay for this place and help you save for college."

She furrowed her brow as she thought about things. "Okay," she said after a moment.

We worked on cleaning up the place for a couple of weeks. Ashla helped us with a lot of the painting. When we were all done and were packing up our tools, she came up to me. "So will you come visit me?"

"Of course," I said. "When you're in college, we will come visit you as much as you want."

"Can I bring my stuff?"

"Yes, you shouldn't take everything to college with you, but you can take what you want," I replied as I put the last of the paint supplies in the car and shut the door.

"Okay, bye," she said and turned around to go back inside.

It dawned on me then that she thought she was going to live here. "You're coming home with us!" I blurted out more forcefully than I meant to. "You aren't living here!"

"But this is my house…" Ashla stated.

"It's a rental. Other people will live here and pay you for it. Just like the people in the basement," I explained. "You don't have to live here. You're too young to move out on your own. Mom and I want you to keep living with us. We wouldn't make you move out."

Relief washed over my daughter's face. "Good, because I really don't want to live here."

Can You Afford to Buy a Home?

There are two things to consider when you ask yourself this question. How much can you afford to pay each month, and how much money do you need to put as a down payment?

Mortgage companies will allow you to have combined monthly debt and housing payments up to 43 percent of your monthly income (as of this writing). This is referred to as a debt-to-income ratio. If you earn $10,000 per month, you can afford $4,300 in debt and housing-related payments. Debt includes any auto loans or leases, credit card payments (only the minimum payment is used in this calculation), student loans, and any other personal debt. Housing payments include the estimated mortgage payment, taxes and insurance, HOA's dues, and private mortgage insurance (PMI). See later in this chapter for more information on these.

This doesn't mean you should accumulate this much debt. If you want to have money for travel, entertainment, and savings, you should try to keep this ratio as low as possible. I think you should keep this less than a third of your gross income, and if you really want to do a lot of other things besides owning a home, than work to keep this below 25 percent of your gross income.

If you are buying a home with a spouse or significant other, their income and debts average into yours. This can help you afford a bigger house. Beware of a partner with bad money management skills, though. Their credit may cause your interest rate to go up, because the lenders see them as riskier to lend to. Also, if your partner's individual debt-to-income ratio is worse than 43 percent when averaged with your own, it will decrease the price of a home you can buy.

The other financial aspect that goes into buying a home is the down payment. Leading up to the Great Recession in 2008, you could buy a home with a bank financing 103 percent of the purchase price. This covered all of the cost of the home, any bank fees, inspections, and appraisals, and gave you some cash to make renovations. You could buy a home and have more money in your pocket after you signed the closing documents.

On the other extreme, I was talking with an investor from Atlanta, Georgia, a few years after the recession had ended. He told me that Atlanta had been one of the worst areas hit by mortgage fraud. To stop the frauds from getting further out of control, all lenders stopped lending in Atlanta for a while.[58] Home purchases in progress stopped, and nobody was buying homes unless they could pay cash. They needed to come up with 100 percent of the purchase price on their own.

I never experienced this and had got my first investment loan in 2007 before the mortgage crisis hit. I bought a property for 10 percent down. A year later, when I was looking at other properties, we had to cough up 30 percent for a down payment, and we were told by a couple of places that they wanted 40 percent down.

During the Great Recession, people could no longer get the PMI. This is an insurance product that helps protect banks and allows them to make loans with less down payment than they normally would. Banks really like borrowers that put 20 percent down. If a borrower has less than this, the bank can still do the loan, but the borrower must pay for the PMI in case they fail to make payments. When a bank takes the property back, the PMI helps cover losses the bank may incur from having to sell the property for less than it previously had sold for and the cost of the legal fees involved from taking a property back.

The only benefit to a borrower for the PMI is that they don't have to come up with as much money for a down payment. The added monthly expense reduces the amount you could otherwise afford as part of your mortgage payment, thus reducing the total amount you could borrow. The PMI has helped a ton of people buy homes that they otherwise couldn't get into. We bought our first home with it. But it is an expense that you should try to eliminate as quickly as possible. See chapter 21 for money saving tips where I describe a few ways to eliminate the PMI.

When my wife and I bought our first home, we put about 8 percent down and paid the loan fees. We had been diligent about saving and my wife had received some money from her grandparents several months earlier to help with college that we hadn't needed at the time. We had the PMI and participated in a state-run first-time home buyer program that required us to attend a class on credit and home ownership that was sponsored by the state. There were plenty of things that we did wrong in that transaction, but I wouldn't change a thing because it helped launch our life together.

---

[58] This may have been a directive coming down from Fannie Mae or some regulatory body. I can't confirm this, but that was the story he told.

Types of Mortgages

A mortgage[59] is a loan that helps you buy a home. There is some variety in the types of mortgages out there, and you should be aware of what they are and what implications they have.

The most common type is a thirty-year fixed-rate mortgage. This loan splits the loan payments up evenly[60] over thirty years with the interest rate staying the same over the entire life of the loan. The payments may still adjust slightly up or down due to taxes and insurance changes that are included into the payment. Most of the time, these adjustments will be upward, but they do occasionally result in a reduction in your payment.

Another common mortgage is very similar to the first, and that is a fifteen-year fixed-rate mortgage. The idea is the same only with your payments being evened out over fifteen years instead. This results in a higher monthly payment. However, oftentimes fifteen-year mortgages have a lower interest rate (not enough to offset for the shorter term) and allow borrowers to pay their loans back much more quickly.

Both the thirty-year and fifteen-year fixed loans are standardized so that banks can sell them to investors. This means you then owe the investors, not the bank. Very often, these loans are sold to Fannie Mae (FNMA).[61] As the biggest buyer of mortgages, Fannie Mae dictates the terms of loans and what documentation is required.

Other types of mortgages are made by portfolio lenders. A portfolio lender is a bank that makes loans that it plans not to sell and wants to keep them and have you continue to make payments to them for your loan. Portfolio lenders structure their loans differently.

Portfolio loans can have an adjustable rate. An ARM stands for Adjustable Rate Mortgage. These types of loans have their interest rate fixed for only predetermined periods. Most often, the rate on an ARM adjusts every five years, but they can adjust more or less frequently. The rate tracks a specific index,[62] such as Treasuries. If when your loan is made and the

---

[59] Mortgages are technically illegal in some states. Those states use what is called a deed of trust instead. However, mortgage is the generally accepted term that most people are familiar with.

[60] This is referred to as amortization. Loans can be amortized over any length of time.

[61] FNMA stands for Federal National Mortgage Association. It is a quasi-governmental company that sets the standards for how loans are structured.

Treasury rate is priced at 1.75 percent and the interest rate on your ARM is 4.75 percent, then you are priced at the Treasury rate plus 3.00 percent. In five years, when your rate adjusts, if the Treasury rate is 2.00 percent, your interest rate will go up to 5.00 percent and your payment will adjust as well.

Since your payment can adjust dramatically, adjustable rates are risky. The benefit to choosing a portfolio lender though is that they oftentimes allow for borrowers that could not otherwise get a mortgage. People who own their own businesses or are considered to be self-employed often have difficulty getting a traditional mortgage due to large fluctuations in income. A portfolio lender may be okay with that. Additionally, if you have recently switched careers or received a large pay raise, a traditional lender may not be able to account for that when determining how much you can borrow. A portfolio lender is more likely to give you credit for a pay increase or forgive a career transition.

There are two other types of mortgages that are far less common. The first is an interest-only mortgage. These were very common prior to the Great Recession. They allowed people to qualify for larger homes, because the lender didn't have to account for how the borrower would repay the principal of the loan so long as they could afford the monthly interest payment.

The other type of an uncommon mortgage has what is called a balloon payment. A loan like this may have the payments split up over thirty years. However, after the first five years, the remaining balance is due. Banks like these loans, as it allows them a mechanism for getting out of the loans that are unprofitable or starting to exhibit signs of greater risk. It forces the borrower to refinance the remaining balance or come up with the cash to pay it off.

Interest-only and balloon-payment mortgages are very uncommon now, but that doesn't mean that you won't see them again.

---

62 An index is a tool that measures a group of securities (stocks), bonds (loans issued to companies), or treasury bonds (loans issued to the government). There are a couple of different indexes. Two common indexes are Treasuries and the Wall Street Journal prime rate, and many banks look to them when determining the pricing of their loans.

Qualifying for a Mortgage

Earlier, I discussed how much you could afford based on your debt-to-income ratio. A bank or a mortgage broker will require documentation to determine your exact debt-to-income ratio. Don't be surprised when they start asking you for dozens of different pieces of documentation. Most commonly, they will request a month's worth of current paystubs showing the income you've earned from your employer and for any co-borrower you may have. They will also request the last two years of tax returns. You will have to complete an application, which will allow the lender to pull your credit report where they will find information about your debts. Depending on what they see on the credit report, they may ask you for recent statements for those debts. If you have negative information on your credit report, they may ask for a letter of explanation.

When I wanted to get loans during the middle of the Great Recession, banks were very demanding in terms of documentation. At that time, they required three years of tax returns, two months' worth of paystubs, and verification of assets—meaning two most recent statements for every checking and savings account I had. Then, since it typically took a month from the time I applied for a loan to the time we actually were able to purchase the house, the bank would require any statements and paystubs that were issued during that time. It was frustrating, but it was just part of the process.

Don't get angry with your lender if they keep requesting information from you. It is just their way of making sure that they make good loans. They also don't want to give you a loan that you can't afford. Such a situation would hurt both you and the bank.

Considerations on Types of Homes

There are different styles of homes you can purchase. The most common home is a single-family residence.[63] This is your basic home that sits on a plot of land by itself. This type of house personifies the typical American dream, but it's not for everybody at all times. It fits a young family with kids very well. It may not work for you if you are young and single and spend more

---

[63] Abbreviated SFR or sometimes SFH for single-family home. These are sometimes called detached homes, as other types of homes are attached to other similar units.

time travelling than you do at home. If you want space and more privacy, a single-family home may be right for you. However, with a larger yard, you are going to be spending more time mowing it or paying someone to do it for you.

A condominium (condo) or a townhome may be more appropriate for you. A condo is a unit where you just own from the walls in. These are very similar to apartments except you own them. A townhome is different from a condo in that you own down to the dirt beneath it and to the sky above it. You may also have a small yard with a townhome. Your neighbors' townhomes are attached to yours like a condo.

A duplex is another type of home. Similar to a townhome, a duplex is two homes that were built attached to each other. There are two ways of owning a duplex. The first is when you can purchase just half of the building (like a townhome), and you own it and the ground beneath it like a single-family home. The other type is when you purchase the entire building. This is beneficial if you want to live in one half and rent the other half out to earn some rental income.[64]

One thing to be aware of when choosing a type of home is the neighborhood Home Owners Association (HOA).[65] They are very good at ensuring the neighborhood is kept clean and well maintained. This could be through citing people for failing to keep up their homes to pre-determined standards or employing landscapers to do yardwork for you. Each HOA is unique, and you should talk to people that live there before moving into any type of home with a HOA.

Make sure you understand the HOA's financial situation. You can review their documentation as a potential resident. You want to know whether the HOA has reserves in place and a plan for any big maintenance items that may come up such as a roof replacement or sidewalk repairs. You can also find out whether the HOA has had any special assessments. A special assessment is an added expense passed onto the residents in the HOA for repairs that were unplanned. If the HOA has not been managed properly, a special

---

[64] There are also triplexes and fourplexes (or quads) that can also be purchased with a regular mortgage. Buildings with more than five units are considered commercial and require a different type of financing.

[65] A neighborhood may be in a metro district, which is similar to an HOA. Without going into too much detail, a metro district gets their funding through special property taxes. They have many of the same duties as an HOA.

assessment may indicate this.

Some homes do not have HOAs at all. Condos, Townhomes, and separate duplexes are almost always governed by a HOA, and many single-family homes are as well. Cities like HOAs, because they enforce a lot of code compliance issues without the city having to get involved. Older neighborhoods and homes outside of city limits are more likely not to have a HOA.

Buying an Old House, a New House, or Building a House

The first rental property I purchased was built in 1873. It was a beautiful old farmhouse with a maid's quarters behind it. The main house was converted into a duplex. It's crazy to think that this house was probably built by someone who lived through the American Civil War. It was old and cold.[66] The electricity to the bathrooms was added at a later point. Due to its age, the house was quirky.

Older homes are more likely to have odd quirks and are likely to be less energy efficient. Older homes require more maintenance and may need major renovations. Some old homes may be dangerous to live in if they still have aluminum wiring.[67] Others may have asbestos, which was mixed into other materials for being an insulation and being fire-resistant, until it was discovered that it is toxic when it is disturbed, and then it becomes extremely dangerous for your lungs. The other major danger found in old homes is lead-based paint, which is a hazard to children when it peels. Lead paint tastes sweet, so small children that tend to stick things in their mouths start ingesting as much as they can find, which leads to lead poisoning.[68]

From a financial standpoint, older homes can sometimes be slightly cheaper per square foot than new homes in the same area. Just be aware of costs of renovation if you think the home will need it while you live there. While you may not notice, you will spend more money fixing small random items in an older home than you would in a new home.

Newly built homes are great because everything is new and you are likely going to have lower maintenance costs. New homes may come with a one-

---

[66] Insulation was not widely available when it was constructed.

[67] Copper wiring is standard. Aluminum wiring was used in the 1960s to the mid-1970s until it was determined that it caused electrical fires.

[68] Lead paint was used in homes built before 1978.

year warranty from the builder so that if something does break the builder will replace or repair it. New homes may be slightly more expensive per square foot than existing homes because of these factors.

In new homes, it is important to pay attention to the quality of construction and the reputation of the builder. While I was in banking, I walked through some new homes that were being built near the bank. Seventy homes were constructed over one summer. It was impressive to watch. However, when I went inside them, I noticed they used very inexpensive cabinets, countertops, light fixtures, and appliances. Paint was applied in a sloppy manner, and I could see screw heads through the paint in the walls. I had a bad feeling about the homes then. And a few years later, I started hearing complaints from the people that moved into them about shoddy craftsmanship. So, just because it's new doesn't mean it is done well.

If you want a new home but aren't finding what you want, building a home may be the route to follow. When you build a home, you can customize the floor plan and finishes. You can also choose your builder and ensure that quality work is done.

Many builders have subdivisions they are building out, with a few different home styles and floor plans to choose from. They also allow a few pre-determined rock and paint colors on the outside but have more flexibility with interior colors.

If you choose to build a home outside of city limits, such as out in the country or mountains, you will likely get away from predetermined house styles and color patterns. You can customize everything to your heart's content.

When building a new home, you may be required to provide construction financing. This is a loan where the builder draws out money from the bank as the work progresses. Unfortunately, you will need to make payments as the home is being built *and* payments on wherever you are living at the time. Alternatively, the bank may allow those payments to be rolled into the loan, in which case, you will then have a larger loan balance to pay back.

Building a new home can be more expensive than purchasing a new home because of the customization options—especially, when you are building outside of a builder's large project subdivision. I once built a spec home with a partner out in the country. We hired a builder to construct the home for us. It took a lot of work to find the right mix of a builder, land, and a home design to produce something we made money on. The home was gorgeous.

The builder told us before we started that it was easier and cheaper to build two homes at once than just one. With two homes or more builders, you can create economies of scale with work crews and purchasing power. This helps keep costs down, which are then passed on to you.

Home Inspections and Appraisals

When we went to buy our first home, I didn't know the difference between the two of these. I figured one person could do both things. How hard could it be to walk through a house, point out everything that's wrong with it, and then tell me how much you think it's worth, right? Oh, keep in mind you have to be highly trained to do both and insured or bonded.[69]

Becoming an inspector is no easy task. It requires between 60 and 200 hours of education and hands-on training. Some states require you to pass a state-specific exam, while others require you to pass a national exam. On top of this, good home inspectors often have a background in construction or other home repair fields.

As tough as it may be to become a home inspector, becoming an appraiser is even harder. Appraisers have more required initial hours of education, ongoing education requirements, and most states require appraisers to apprentice for a few years under another appraiser.

Another reason why an inspector can't also be an appraiser is because the inspector works for you as the buyer, and the appraiser works for the bank. Banks have many regulations they must follow, and having an appraiser work for, and be paid by, them is critical to making sure that the appraiser's interests are aligned with the bank's interests. While an inspector and an appraiser may note some of the same things in their reports, they are trying to protect different people.

I didn't know any of this when we bought our first home, but my real estate agent did, so he set me up with a home inspector. He came out, and I followed the guy around the house. He pointed out all the little things that we had wrong with the house, and told me not to worry about some things when I had questions. We spent about two hours at the house, and it cost us a few hundred dollars. He was very knowledgeable, and I felt like I got my money's worth.

---

[69] Bonded is another way of providing reimbursement to a business' customer. To you as a customer, it is similar to insurance.

What that inspector didn't do was a sewer inspection. At the time, most inspectors didn't do them. Had I known how big a deal this would be later, I would have used a company, such as Roto Rooter, to come out and run a camera down the sewer line.[70]

Recently, my wife and I bought a new home and hired a guy I had met through work to do the inspection. He was more expensive. But instead of spending a couple hours at the property, he spent half a day. He was so thorough that I got bored and left to go back to work for a few hours. In addition to a normal inspection, he also did a sewer line inspection and sent it to me electronically. While I thought he was expensive, having one person inspect the home and the sewer line ended up costing about the same as paying one person for the home inspection and another person to inspect the sewer line.

If you are buying a new(er) home, you may feel comfortable with not getting a sewer inspection. They may not even be common in your area. The problem we ran into here was that for a time around the fifties and sixties they used clay pipes for sewer lines. Tree roots can easily break through clay pipes, especially at the joints. Even more modern PVC pipes can have issues with tree roots growing through the joints. For this reason, I always recommend the added expense of getting a sewer line inspection.

I like to meet the inspector when they are going through a house. I get a better feel for the inspector and a better feel for the home. There have been times when I haven't,[71] specifically when I have purchased rentals out of state.

I have never met an appraiser when they were walking though a house. Not even my own house when I was selling it. They are working for the bank, and they don't really need or want any input from the buyer or seller unless it is technical information about the house. So don't be surprised if you don't get to meet the person that determines how much the home is worth.

---

[70] After having sewer line problems at my own house and then at one of my first rentals, I had Roto Rooter do a sewer line inspection at every other house that I purchased.

[71] One time, I couldn't get off work to meet an inspector for a house I was purchasing close by. Since I'd used him before though, I trusted the report I would get from him would be thorough.

Closing on a Home and Two Types of Escrow

Escrow is a term you may not have heard if you've never owned a home. Escrow is money held by an impartial third party on behalf of you and someone else.

When you put an offer on a home and it is accepted, you are required to put down earnest money. Earnest money is a portion of the down payment typically ranging from $1,000 to $5,000 that you will deposit with a title company or a title lawyer.[72] Depositing this money with the title company is called opening escrow. The title company holds the money in good faith until you either complete the purchase of the home or back out of the contract to purchase.

When you complete the purchase, you bring the rest of your down payment to the title company. The bank shows up with their loan documents for you to sign and the money they are lending you for the purchase. The title company or lawyer will have prepared the state-required paperwork to transfer ownership of the home. You sign all the paperwork, and the seller signs the paperwork to transfer ownership to you. The seller walks away with the money (after paying off any mortgage that they had on the home), and you walk away with the keys to your new home. Congratulations!

This closes out that escrow account.

Now you have a new escrow account. Banks found out a long time ago that it was really important for people to pay their property taxes and insurance. Insurance protects the owner and the bank in case of a disaster. Without it, a home may burn down, with no money for it to get replaced. The borrower would still owe the money, but the home would be gone. There would be little incentive for the borrower to keep paying, and then the bank would be stuck with a burned down home that wasn't worth what was still owed on it.

Property taxes are something else banks are very interested in having people pay. Property taxes supersede[73] a bank's lien position, meaning that a

---

[72] Some states allow real estate transactions to be closed (meaning completed) by title companies. Others require that the process be overseen by a competent attorney.

[73] In this case, *superseded* means that property taxes are more important than a bank loan at all times. In the event that the property is foreclosed on and sold, the property taxes get paid first, then the loan, even though the property taxes that are due occurred after the loan had been made.

home can be taken from a borrower by the government for failing to pay their property taxes. When this happens, a bank loses the home as collateral for their loan. When this occurs, banks may cough up the money to keep the home themselves rather than lose more money.

To combat this, banks began requiring escrow payments rolled into their monthly loan payments. Banks would figure out how much the insurance was for a year and how much property taxes were estimated to be. They would add those two together and divide it by twelve. That amount was included with the loan payment.

The money isn't paid immediately for insurance and taxes though. It accumulates in an escrow account until both are due. If there is any shortage, the bank reassesses what you should be paying for the next year to make up the difference.

In the event you overpay your escrow account significantly, the bank may be required to issue the money back to you. This is uncommon, but it does happen. Sometimes it is the result of your making changes to your insurance, which results in a lower premium (cost). When home values fell in 2008 and 2009, property taxes also came down dramatically. This led to some escrow money being returned to homeowners.

Time to Move

You've bought your first home! Congratulations! You should be proud of yourself!

Now comes the work…

Moving is not a fun task. More than likely, you have been getting ready to move while you were also waiting to close on your new home. Hopefully, you've been packing and getting rid of unwanted or unnecessary stuff already. If not, you've got a lot left to do.

Chances are you are young, full of energy, and don't have too much stuff (at least compared to how much stuff you will have later in life). So, you should move yourself.

Moving companies are expensive. Moving across town can cost $300 to $1,500 easily. Moving to a different state can cost several thousand dollars. It is not uncommon for it to cost as much as $10,000.

A better option is to rent a U-haul or other truck and do it yourself. Renting a small cargo truck currently costs less than $50 a day and is likely to be closer to $20. Moving across the country, when you will not be returning the vehicle to the same place you picked it up, can vary widely in price, depending on where the vehicles are needed. However, you are talking hundreds of dollars, not thousands like a professional moving company.

The cheapest option is to do it all yourself, preferably with friends. Hopefully, you know at least one person with a truck you can borrow. I recommend pizza and beer for your friends as a thank you.

Home Repairs

The biggest financial difference between owning and renting a home is that now doing any repairs is your business. When you are a renter, a backed-up sink or a fridge that breaks down would be dealt with by the landlord. As a homeowner, you get to pay for these things now.

We live in a great time period. You can learn how to do any type of home repair on YouTube. If you've got any familiarity with tools at all, you can handle the majority of small home repairs that come your way.

Unless you are pretty handy, I wouldn't recommend taking on major remodels, but minor things such as fixing a sink are easy to do. It's also easy to find online videos instructing how to do it. My daughter knows a lot about making minor repairs, as she has helped me on a number of occasions. These are small skills that will help her save money the rest of her life, because she won't have to pay anyone else to do it.

For big projects and projects you are uncomfortable with, you should pay a professional. I've fixed dishwashers and other appliances by watching videos online. I struggle with them every time, and it takes me forever to do. On top of that, six months after I fix it, something else breaks, leaving me to wonder whether I did something wrong or should have just replaced the appliance when it first broke.

Some unexpected repairs will also be covered by insurance. A roof damaged by hail is a major one that occurs frequently where I live in Colorado. I am liable for my deductible of $2,500 only, and the insurance company covers the rest of the $15,000 roof replacement. It is required by both the insurance company and by the county inspector that a licensed roofer complete the job (see chapter 15 for more information on insurance.)

You Will Sell the Home Someday

Rebecca and I once painted an accent wall in our kitchen the color of pea soup. It was hideous but we loved it. For us, we thought, it went really well with the brown cabinets. We also hung a large picture on that wall, which was also complimented by the color. We knew before we painted it that if we ever moved, we would have to paint that wall again.

Sure enough, six years later we were moving out. We had shown our realtor the house before we did much to get it ready to sell. He walked in, saw the wall, and asked whether we were planning on painting. Being snarky, we told him no and that the wall was beautiful and that we couldn't imagine painting over it.

After a nervous look crossed his face, we had a good laugh and painted over the wall the next week.

The ugly wall brought us joy for six years. We had a lot of conversations about how ugly it was amongst ourselves and with visitors. We loved it, but we never once thought anyone else would like it. Everyone who saw the wall was horrified by the color.

For the cost of a can of paint and an hour or two of work, we got a lot of enjoyment out of the wall. For the cost of another can of paint and another couple hours of work, we painted over it so the house would actually sell.

Paint can be changed easily. Light fixtures are another thing that can be changed pretty quickly and easily without needing to pay someone else to do it. Other things are harder to change.

When we moved into that same house, the bathroom had the seventies' green tile, and the tub, toilet, and sink were all pink. Remodeling the bathroom took much longer than painting the wall. I had the ability to do it myself, so I did. It took about three weeks to get done, because I had to work on it around my work schedule. When we changed it, we went with much more universally appealing colors.

Feel free to experiment all you want with easily changeable things like paint. Use a little more discretion when installing semi-permanent items. A kitchen may be remodeled once every twenty–forty years and is very expensive. If done just to suit your personal tastes, it may also decrease the value of your home.

Why I Want My Daughter to Know This

After a year of renting a place, we received a letter from a mortgage broker[74]

---

[74] A mortgage broker is a person or company that does not work for a bank but

talking about getting into our first home. It seemed like good timing, as our lease was almost up. We didn't know anything about buying a home back then, and the letter made a lot of promises. We set an appointment with the guy and went into his office with the intent to learn all we could.

We walked in. We were both twenty years old and looked younger. The gentleman wasn't rude, but he definitely dismissed us outright. He told us he couldn't do anything for us. We needed to work for a couple mire years to establish better work histories and credit. (He didn't pull our credit, so I don't know how he knew what it looked like.) He did tell us to keep saving money and that we had a decent start on savings.

About four months passed by, and there was a first-time home buyer class advertised at the college. We were now very curious about buying a home, so we signed up. The class consisted of my wife, me, and one other guy that was our age. It was taught by a real estate agent and a mortgage broker that had teamed up.

I couldn't tell you what we learned in the class itself. I know their presentation was about forty-five minutes long, and the other guy in the class split as soon as it was over. The real estate agent and the mortgage broker both sat down with us to talk about what our goals were.

We told them we had already talked to one mortgage broker and that we needed a couple of years more under our belt before we could buy a home. We were content with waiting and just doing and learning everything we could so that we would eventually be able to buy our own home.

They both told us the previous guy was wrong. They explained to us some first-time home buyer programs that were out there. They set an appointment for us to meet with the mortgage broker to see whether we could get prequalified.

We felt a little silly but gathered up our paystubs from our jobs and the one tax return we had filed together and went to meet with her. We left the meeting knowing that we could buy a home and how much we could afford.

The real estate agent then started showing us homes. He showed us six small homes in the area we wanted to live (close to the college so we could finish school easily). When we found one we really liked, he helped us put an offer together on it.

---

makes mortgage loans. They can work with specific mortgage companies, or they can work with several mortgage companies and banks to try to give you several loan options.

Six weeks after attending the class, we purchased our first home. We were so happy and proud! The other guy dismissed us outright and told us to call him when we thought we were actually ready to buy a home.

From this experience, we learned that a "no" with one person doesn't mean it can't be done. We also learned that you shouldn't be dismissive of people when you think they don't matter. Our real estate agent on that deal ended up helping us buy four investment properties as well and helped us sell a flip that we bought. He ended up getting six sales commissions out of us over about twelve years.[75]

If you are wanting to buy your first home, be open to learning and take advantage of any classes you can. Talk to mortgage brokers and real estate agents when you get the chance. They may help you achieve your dreams much sooner than you thought possible.

---

[75] I still highly recommend him and stopped using him only because a friend of mine got their license and I partnered with him on a deal.

15: INSURANCE

"What were you doing today, Dad?" Ashla asked as I walked in the door. I was working from home at the time, so she was used to my being home when she got home from school.

"I had to meet with the roofer to get him started on putting new roofs on our rentals here," I said as I set down my things. "He is meeting the insurance adjuster next week."

"What's an insurance adjuster?"

"A person that works for the insurance company that determines whether you can make a claim and how much."

She looked at me puzzled.

"You know what insurance is, right?" I asked.

"Well, kind of…"

"Ok, so insurance is a pool of money that you and a bunch of other people pay into. If you have an emergency, you can pull back out that money, the money it has earned in interest, and sometimes other people's money. You don't have control over it like a savings account, but you can potentially pull more out than you put into it."

I continued, "You make a claim when you have an accident, and something is damaged. With our rentals, the roofs were damaged by hail. Over the time we've owned these properties, we've paid over $40,000 in insurance just for them. The roofs are going to cost over $70,000, and our portion of that is about $15,000. So, we are getting back an extra $15,000 from the insurance company."

"So how do they make money?" she asked.

"Well, we have more rentals we aren't making claims on that we've paid on that have never had a claim. They have also been able to take all the money we've paid in and invest it to earn interest and dividends. So, they can cover our claims easily and make money."

"So why don't we just save the money and cover it ourselves?" she asked.

"It's taken ten years to pay in $40,000. If just one of those places burned down, we would be looking at about $300,000 to rebuild it. That is something that would be extremely difficult to save up for. It's also extremely rare, but it could happen."

Before we get into each type of insurance, there are a few definitions you should know. The first is **premium**, which is how much the insurance costs you each month or year. The second is **deductible**, which is how much you must pay out of pocket before insurance starts paying the rest. Similar to a deductible is a **co-pay**. This is specific to health insurance and means how much you pay directly for routine services like a checkup or flu shot. A co-pay is less than your deductible, but it is a predetermined amount set by the insurance and their network of hospitals as to what you should be paying.

A trick that auto and homeowner's insurance companies like to use to determine whether they can insure you and how much they should charge you is to look at your history of making claims. All the claims you make are recorded and usually shared among insurance companies so they can see whether a person is likely to have a lot of accidents. While you may expect your monthly auto insurance costs to go up if you cause an accident and make a claim, what you don't expect is that your homeowner's insurance premiums will also go up. Yet this very thing happens a lot. This doesn't even have to be with the same company. Insurance companies all have access to a lot of the same data, so if one reports a claim you made on your auto insurance policy, another company may raise your homeowner's insurance. Your claims and accidents stay with you for several years, and you are unlikely to see a decline in the costs of your insurance.

Further, insurance companies may deny you for coverage, based on old claims. My wife once got in a fender-bender with a truck we owned for a short time. Two years and nine months later, I was denied coverage for a rental property I was purchasing, because we had too many claims recently. I was told that I couldn't get coverage until that claim was more than three years old. I used a different company for four months and then re-applied with the first company (because they had lower rates). I was accepted without a problem.

Insurance is a complex subject with many different companies providing a variety of products for you to choose from. What follows is a description of the common types of insurance you can obtain and what you should know about them.

Auto

Car insurance is required by most states. Many dealerships cannot even sell you a car without your being able to obtain a proof of insurance. There are two primary types of car insurance: liability and full coverage.

Liability insurance covers the damage you would cause to other people or property in the event you cause an accident. **Full Coverage** is the damage you cause to your own vehicle. It is possible to get just liability insurance, and this is the minimum that is often required by states. Full coverage is optional (unless you have a loan on the car and the lender requires it). It pays for repairs or replacement of the vehicle up to the value that the insurance company determines.

Inside of your liability insurance, you will want to pay attention to the amount that is covered in the event you do bodily injury to others or damage property. These are typically listed separately. Bodily injury to others is then further broken down to how much is covered per person and how much is covered per accident. For instance, you may have $100,000 coverage per person and $200,000 per accident. Damage to property is considered separately. So, your insurance may pay out $100,000 to damage done to a person and then another $25,000 for damage done to their vehicle or other property.

How much coverage you think you should carry is up to you, and the insurance company is prohibited from giving you too much guidance on this. There is a lot of advice on the Internet as to how much coverage people think you should carry. For me, I want enough that it should fully pay for a couple of people to spend a week in the hospital. Whatever you think that number is, then that's how much you should have.

It has always been my preference to carry full coverage on all my vehicles because in the event of an accident I wanted them fixed or replaced. But when I did the math, I realized it was cheaper to get liability only coverage which would save me money that I could put into a savings account for a vehicle in the future. Our old Scion Xb is worth only about $1,500 now, and our deductible is $500, so if we get in an accident, the most the insurance company will pay is $1,000. I thought this sounded like a good deal but I realized it cost almost $40 a month more than liability only coverage. By opting for liability only coverage, in two years, we will have saved nearly that $1,000 ($40 x 12months x 2years=$960) that could be put towards replacing the vehicle.

Other considerations that weigh into the cost of your auto insurance are things like accident forgiveness, which you can pay for ahead of time, or just avoiding accidents for several years. Rental car reimbursement covers the cost of your rental car while your car is in the shop. Towing and labor (often called roadside assistance) pays for a tow, help changing a flat tire, or delivery of gas. Many of these are optional, and it is up to you to decide whether you want to pay for them.

Another item that affects your cost (that you can control) is what your deductible is. In the event of an accident, how much money do you have saved to pay for repairs before you want insurance to step in and cover the rest? The lower your deductible the higher the costs. If you don't have much in savings, then it is probably worth having a lower deductible, even though your monthly premium will be higher.

How many accidents you've had recently will play a big factor in your insurance costs. If the insurance company thinks you are a bad driver, then your insurance costs will go up. If you've had a recent claim, then the insurance company wants to both guard against another claim and help reimburse some of the costs of the last claim. The accident forgiveness coverage mentioned above helps protect you from a sudden increase in your monthly premium due to an accident.

Renters'

If you have moved out of your parents' place and don't own your home yet, then chances are you're renting (although homelessness is an option). Your landlord has an insurance policy that will cover his building in the event of a fire or another disaster. The landlord's insurance doesn't protect you!

If the place burns down or is broken into, and you lose all your stuff and don't have renters insurance, then it stinks to be you.

Renter's insurance is a very inexpensive product, which helps replace your stuff. Additionally, it covers your liability if a visitor to the property is injured through your negligence. This can help pay for medical bills if someone trips over a bike you (or your kid) left lying in the driveway.

Renter's insurance is typically pretty cheap and easy to obtain.

Health

Health insurance is a monster and can be extremely difficult to understand. I will do my best to break it down. There are several types of health insurance that you can choose from.

Traditional Indemnity Plan (Fee-for-Service Plan) – Structured like auto insurance coverage, this type of insurance requires a deductible to be paid before additional services are paid for by the insurance company. Often, they have an 80/20 cost sharing for medical expenses. This means that once you fulfill your deductible requirements, the insurance company picks up 80 percent of the cost and you are still liable for 20 percent. This can be a scary thought, but they also typically have out-of-pocket caps, and once you exceed that number, then the insurance picks up 100 percent.

Recently, someone I know was diagnosed with a major illness, and they have this type of insurance. Their insurance has a $1,500 deductible and costs are split 80/20 after that. Given the type of illness, they were still concerned that their 20 percent would be $10,000 or more per year with treatment likely to continue for many years. However, their out-of-pocket expenses are capped at $3,600 per year. Learning about this cap took a ton of stress off them and their family.

High-Deductible Health Insurance – Varying in structure from the traditional indemnity plan is the high-deductible health insurance. Rather than having caps and 80/20s, the high-deductible plan starts you out with a maximum out-of-pocket every year. The number is high, sometimes a scary amount, but once you hit that amount, the insurance company pays for the rest. If you are young and healthy, this may be a great way to save money. This type of plan is typically cheaper, and the government allows for it to be paired with a Health Savings Account (HSA). A health savings account lets you contribute money tax free so long as the money is used for qualified health-related expenses. If you are maximizing your other retirement savings options an HSA can allow you to save even more tax-free money now. Later in life, you can use those funds when you are likely to have more health expenses. So long as the funds are only used for medical expenses, no taxes are paid on the money or any interest that it earns.

Preferred Provider Organizations (PPOs) – These organizations have made arrangements with a variety of doctors for pre-determined costs for services. These costs to you are lower than if you were to pay for the services yourself, and they are generally considered cheaper for the insurance company as well. The cost to you up front is your **co-pay**. The doctors and medical organizations that have agreed to these cost-structuring plans are considered to be **in network**. However, there are many doctors that have not agreed to the insurance company's predetermined cost structure. These doctors are referred to as **out of network**. For an out-of-network provider, you would have to pay the entire bill up front and then submit receipts to your insurance company. The insurance company is likely to reimburse up to 80 percent of the cost.

PPOs allow you to go directly to a specialist,[76] as long as it is an in-network provider, without needing pre-approval from the insurance company or seeing a primary care physical first to get a referral. You are strongly incentivized to stay within the network due to the reduced costs and easier paperwork.

A variant of the PPO is the EPO or **exclusive provider organization**. This type of organization pays for services provided only in network.

Point-of-service (POS) – These are similar to PPOs except that they rely strongly on a primary care physician.[77] You are required to see a primary care physician prior to a visit to a specialist. If your primary care physician recommends you to a doctor that is out of network, the POS is more likely to pick up most of the costs (once you exceed your deductible). A POS plan is more likely to cover preventive care services and improvement programs such as smoking cessation.

Health Maintenance Organizations (HMOs) – HMOs are often the least expensive plans, but they are also the least flexible. Often, they work with members of group plans (like a large group of people insured by an employer) more than with individuals. They require referrals from a primary care physician to see a specialist and may require pre-approval before you visit an emergency room (which can be achieved with a phone call). HMOs may wholly own medical offices and employ the doctors and nurses you will see regularly, or they may consist of a network of individual practices similar to

---

[76] A specialist is a doctor that focuses only on one area of medicine. For example, a gastroenterologist focuses on the digestive system. You wouldn't want to ask them a question about your acne.

[77] A primary care physician, sometimes referred to as a PCP, is usually a doctor that you designate as your regular doctor. They handle annual checkups and most of your non-emergency health needs. They also have the power to refer you to specialists—doctors that don't work as PCPs and instead focus on a single area (such as brain surgeons).

the other plans. They are unlikely to pay for doctors outside the network. HMOs are most likely to cover preventive care services and health improvement programs.

Medical Cost Sharing – Medical cost sharing operates similarly to credit unions (see chapter 4) when a group of people have gotten together and create their own pool of funds to share amongst themselves for medical expenses. Their structure is often similar to high-deductible health insurance in that you have a large deductible to meet before you can dip into the community savings. A large difference is that the deductible for medical cost sharing is *per event*, whereas other deductibles are *per year*. If you have a couple of medical events each year, you have to reach your deductible each time.

Cost-sharing plans don't offer co-pays or free services anywhere. However, they do provide education on how to pay your bills as a *cash payer* and then help you negotiate larger bills. They work to keep their overhead and payouts very low and then pass these savings to their members. When I transitioned out of the workplace to start my own business, I had to find my own insurance. I ended up going with a medical cost-sharing plan, because I had a bunch of savings in an old HSA[78] (see High Deductible Health Insurance earlier in this chapter for information on HSAs) that I could tap in the event of an emergency. The cost of the medical cost-sharing plan was about a third of the cost of the high-deductible health insurance plan I was also considering.

Homeowners

When buying a home with a mortgage, you will be required to get homeowners insurance with certain minimum coverages dictated by the bank. A homeowner's policy covers damage to your home through internal mishaps like a kitchen fire, external disasters like a tornado, and the actions of others such as theft.

Like with other insurance policies, you will be able to choose your deductible. However, with homeowners the deductible is typically more than what you would have for an auto policy. Deductibles on homeowner policies can be a little convoluted. In recent years, insurance companies have been

---

[78] Unless specifically allowed, medical cost sharing does not allow you to contribute to an HSA; however, you can use previously saved funds towards medical expenses.

splitting out the deductible for wind and hail. This is common practice where I live in Colorado, especially since the insurance companies nicknamed my region "hail alley." This split deductible means that all other covered losses have a standard deductible (I chose $2,000), and damage from wind and hail has a higher deductible (mine is $3,000). I could have had a lower wind and hail deductible, but my premium would have gone up significantly.

Insurance companies will have many preset deductibles that you can choose from, which are typically in increments of $500 to $1,000. They have also come out with a percentage of value deductibles. These deductibles are vague and are based on how much an insurance company determines your home is worth at the time of the incident.

One time, my insurance company switched me from a flat $1,000 deductible to a 2 percent deductible without my being aware of it. I went to make a claim and ended up cancelling the claim because my deductible had jumped up to about $4,000, which was just more than I expected the total value of the claim would be.

What I learned is that you should review your insurance policies at least once a year. The insurance company had slipped in the change in deductible into annual forms they emailed out that I didn't read. They allowed me to change it back to a flat deductible; however, since the incident was in the past, it could not be covered at the new lower insurance deductible amount.

I strongly prefer having a set deductible rather than a floating percentage. In the event of a disaster, I know exactly what I need to come up with for my deductible. The percentage had a cheaper monthly premium, but my deductible ended up being a weird amount and much higher than I was thinking it would be. My background in banking has made me risk adverse on certain things, and having a floating deductible is one element of risk you can easily eliminate.

One other thing to be aware of is that homeowner's insurance covers only from the walls in. Anything that happens in your sewer line is not covered. I can tell you that was a nasty surprise.[79]

---

[79] The insurance company did cover the damage done inside the home due to the sewer backup. However, replacing the damaged sewer line came out of my pocket.

Disability

Disability insurance is often referred to as disability income protection, as it covers you in the event you suffer a disability that hampers your ability to work and earn income. This could be short term (like a broken leg) or long term (such as a traumatic brain injury). Short-term disability insurance covers you for up to six months, while long-term disability insurance is designed to last for more than six months and likely could mean the rest of your life.

Short-term disability insurance can replace 60–70 percent of your base salary and usually pays out for just a few months (some policies pay longer than others). If these policies have a waiting period, it is usually less than a month from the point that a disability occurs.

Long-term disability insurance replaces 40–60 percent of your base salary. The payments end either when the disability ends or after a number of years, depending on the policy. Sometimes the benefits may last all the way until you reach retirement age. Often, these have a waiting period of 90 days before the insurance company begins making payments to you.

Your employer may provide you with either short-term or long-term disability insurance, or maybe even both. A few states already require that employers provide disability insurance. If you live in a state that doesn't and work for an employer who doesn't, then you can buy disability insurance through a number of providers. Your employer may have an agreement with a provider whereby you can purchase disability insurance more cheaply than you could through finding a provider on the Internet. If you are a member of any professional organization, they may also offer you disability insurance at a discount.

In the event you choose not to get disability insurance, make sure you build up your savings account. If you are out of work for a few months with an injury, you should be able to survive off your savings.

The government also offers a safety net in the form of Supplemental Security Income (SSI). If you are working, then you are already contributing to this in the form of social security withholdings. This method of receiving income as the result of a disability is less than ideal, as payments can be less than you would hope for. However, you should be aware that it does exist should the worst happen.

Life

Life insurance is the one thing nobody wants to talk about, because nobody wants to confront their own mortality. Life insurance isn't for you; it's for the ones you leave behind. In the event of your death, whom do you want to protect from the loss of your income? Most often, this is children and a spouse or even other family members that may rely on you financially.

If you are young, single, and childless, then life insurance may not be something you care about or even really need. As you start building a family, life insurance becomes more important. A general rule of thumb is to get life insurance equal to two times your annual income. This would protect your loved ones for two years after you pass away. I followed this advice for a time but soon realized that it wasn't enough for me to feel secure. With our real estate investments and businesses I wanted enough life insurance that if I were to pass away, there would be enough money to pay off all the loans on rental properties, businesses, and our own home mortgage.

As a commercial lender, I would often require my business owners to get life insurance regardless of whether they had family. Usually, I required enough to pay off their loan, but I didn't necessarily require the money to be used for that. The mentality was that if a key owner passed away revenues could decline, while the expense of replacing that person could lead to payroll costs going up. A business should have a pool of money to dip into in the event an owner passes away. In this scenario, you are protecting all the people that work for you.

I find life insurance to be one of the most complicated because there are so many options available. Whereas you may get an insurance policy for a home and expect that policy to be perpetual so long as you keep making payments, life insurance doesn't necessarily work that way.

Term life insurance is a policy that lasts for only a set number of years. I like this policy a lot for business owners that are constantly growing their business, starting new businesses, and buying assets such as real estate. If your life is constantly changing, a term policy may be a good choice because you are forced to re-evaluate your life every so often and determine whether you are carrying enough life insurance. Term policies are generally cheaper than other policies, especially if you are young and in good health.

I also have a **whole life insurance** policy. Whole Life acts more like a permanent policy. Your payments are more than they would be with a term policy, sometimes as much as five to fifteen times more than a term life policy with the same dollar amount for your death benefit. These types of policies sometimes have a neat feature whereby they accumulate a cash value. A **cash value** is almost like a savings account. It lies within the policy whereby part of the premium you pay each month is set aside with the insurance company in an account for you and earns interest. It can take a while for the cash value to accumulate, and different policies have different fees that affect the rate at which your policy may accumulate cash value. You are paid interest on the cash value, which is then credited to your account.

Universal life insurance is very similar to whole life except that the policy holder can change the premium and death benefit amounts without needing to get a new policy. Universal life is also subject to market rate[80] interest rates on the cash value portion. So, if the rate decreases too much, you may need to pay a higher premium to keep up with the fees.

Another option is **variable life insurance**, which is similar to whole life insurance in that it has a cash value function. With a whole life policy, the interest rate is similar to a savings account, whereas variable life allows you to invest your cash value into a series of mutual funds, thus exposing you to higher potential returns (and potential losses) that come with investing in the stock market.

If you combine universal life and variable life you come up with **variable universal life insurance**. Variable universal life allows you to adjust the premiums and death benefit (like universal life) while also allowing you to invest the funds into a set of mutual funds. The exposure of both variable life and variable universal life to mutual funds means that you run the risk of expensive monthly policy premiums with the possibility of no cash value earning interest to help pay for those premiums.

When you go to apply for life insurance, you typically also have to participate in some sort of medical exam. Sometimes, this requires visiting a doctor that the life insurance company specifies. It can be as simple as having a travel nurse come to your home or office and take blood samples for their lab to run tests on. You can bypass this medical exam with **simplified issue life insurance.** You are still likely to be required to complete a medical questionnaire (which all policies will subject you to). Simplified issue life insurance can allow you to obtain life insurance more quickly as well as avoid needles if you are uncomfortable with them. Simplified issue can still be very

---

[80] Market rate refers to a percentage return (rate) that can be accessed by everyone (the market).

affordable.

A way to skip the medical questionnaire would be to get a **guaranteed issue life insurance**. These policies are expensive, but they can be very appealing to the elderly and those in poor health, as you cannot be denied coverage under this type of policy. Due to the added risk to the insurance company, the monthly premiums for these policies are much more expensive than other options.

If you are confused by all this, you are not alone. If you are working for someone else, hopefully they have a **group life insurance** policy that they either provide to you as an employee or you can buy into. When I worked in banking, my employer provided life insurance equal to two times my salary at no cost to me with the option to purchase additional insurance if I chose to.

Identity Theft

I discuss identity theft more in chapter 19. Simply put, it is when someone obtains enough information about you to open up credit cards or take out loans in your name. If it happens to you, it is a big pain in the butt to fix. You can spend hours on the phone and Internet, talking to companies, explaining the situation, and getting them to remove fraudulent[81] items out of your name and off your credit report. Often, you don't realize your identity has been stolen until you attempt to take out credit for a purchase of your own, such as buying a home or a car.

It can take a few months to clean everything up. Identity theft insurance does all the clean-up for you. Often, they provide credit-monitoring services as well. This allows them and you to know when suspicious activity occurs in your name. It helps them get ahead of the game when it comes to shutting down fraudulent accounts.

Identity theft insurance is fairly inexpensive and can provide a lot of peace of mind.

Why I Want My Daughter to Know This

Insurance is one of the topics that I always find the most confusing. I feel like there is no one resource to turn to in order to get all your options on any type

---

[81] Here, *fraudulent* means credit cards, loans, or other accounts that were opened up in your name by criminals.

of insurance (except for maybe car insurance). Life insurance companies may not have all the types of life insurance available to even offer them to you. Insurance brokers are aware of the intricacies of the policies offered by only those companies that they work with. You may have more options and not even be aware of it.

The other thing I find aggravating is that it is impossible to have all your insurance needs be met by a single company. I like that with banking you can get all your needs met (for the most part) by a single bank. Need a personal checking account? Done. Need a business account? Done. What about a health savings account? No problem.

Compare that to the insurance industry, which is heavily fragmented. Insurance companies love to bundle auto and homeowners insurance, but that's about it. My health insurance (which is a medical cost-sharing plan) is through one company, while my auto and home insurance are through another. The company that insures my home allows a person to have only a few rental properties and at a much higher cost. So, all of my rental properties are insured through yet another company. I have a whole life policy through one company but have a term life through yet another company, which was my choice because of the cost. I don't currently have disability insurance. But if I chose to get it, I would have to engage yet another company.

I hope this chapter provides a bit of illumination on the subject of insurance, without making your eyes glaze over. When shopping around for insurance, you should know a little bit about the different types of insurance available in order to compare apples to apples.

16: RETIREMENT INVESTING

"Why do you guys invest in houses?" Ashla asked.

"We want to have money coming in other than what we get from our jobs. We want to quit our jobs and be able to still have nice things, travel, and do fun things. We want to retire early and enjoy our life doing the things we want."

She thought this over for a moment and then asked, "Is that the only way to do that?"

"No. Everyone should be investing money for retirement. Your Mom and I have just been more aggressive than others about it. Most people invest in the stock market, which is like owning tiny bits of many companies, as a way to save money for retirement. You can earn more this way than with a savings account. Some people also own rental properties, like we do, so they can receive income for when they retire. Others also own their own companies and plan on selling them to fund their retirement. There are many ways you can have money to retire on."

"So why do you work?"

"Right now, we don't have enough money coming in from our investments for us to quit. Once we do, we will quit."

"Who will quit first?" Ashla asked.

I considered it for a moment. "Probably me. Your Mom really likes working, and she really loves her job."

"I hope Mom quits first."

As the Chinese proverb says, "The best time to plant a tree was twenty years ago. The second best time to plant a tree is today."

I don't have many quotations in this book, but this one I love, and it summarizes retirement investing so simply. As they say, hindsight is 20/20,[82]

---

[82] Hindsight is 20/20" is a common phrase referring to looking back and having perfect vision, respectively. So looking back you can see what you should have done for everything to come out perfect. It's easier to see what should have happened, compared to trying to predict what may happen ahead of time.

which is why it would have been so much better to start saving for retirement twenty years ago just as it would have been to plant a tree twenty years ago. If you haven't done this, then start right now.

I've been very successful investing in real estate for the long term. I also got lucky with my timing (even though it didn't feel very lucky most of the time). I believe firmly that anyone can become a millionaire or more if they are consistent about saving and investing, and they start early enough.

It was a common myth when I was growing up that if you invested 10 percent of your income from the time you started working at fifteen, you could retire by the time you were thirty-five. This would be very hard to accomplish.[83] But by starting to save early, you have time on your side.

Sadly, I didn't save 10 percent of my income to try this out. Looking back at my old tax returns, I don't think I had a million dollars in *lifetime* earnings from a job by the time I turned thirty-five. So it may have been very difficult to save enough to retire by thirty-five, using traditional methods only. Since I combined my retirement savings with some real estate investing, it did allow me to leave a job at the age of thirty-five, though I did still need to start a business to fund my desired lifestyle.

I think that once a person starts working, they can't wait for the day when they get to stop. Planning for retirement should begin as early as possible so you have time on your side.

A 401(k) Is a Retirement Account, not an Ultramarathon

The moment you start working, you may already be eligible to start saving for retirement. Many employers offer their employees a 401(k). This is a retirement account set up by the employer when employees can direct a portion of their *pre-tax* income. This can lessen tax consequences on employees while allowing them to save towards their retirement.

There is no minimum age for 401(k) accounts; however, employers are not legally required to include employees in their plan until they reach the age of twenty-one. Many times, part-time employees will not qualify to participate

---

[83] The problem with this is that you are trying to save 10 percent of your income at a time in your life when you earn very little and likely need most of it for living expenses. Also, that 10 percent is very low and will take a long time to grow, and twenty years is not very long. If this were true, you could also start at thirty-five and retire at fifty-five, which is still early retirement by most standards.

in the plan, and often small employers do not even have 401(k) plans set up for their employees.

If you get a job that has a 401(k), you should immediately start taking advantage of it because of the ability to save money before the government takes a portion for taxes. At the time of this writing, you can contribute up to $19,500 into a 401(k) per year. Once you get to be fifty years old, you can contribute an extra $6,500. These amounts adjust upwards fairly frequently, so you can save quite a bit of money here.

Until I was in my thirties, saving that much money seemed like a joke. I had a family, a mortgage, student loan debt, and my income was less than $40k (and my wife made about the same). We were saving, but the idea of each of us saving half of our paycheck was unrealistic. We both saved some, and when we worked at jobs that offered an employer match, we made sure to save enough to take advantage of that.

An **employer match** is when an employer contributes an amount to your 401(k), based on what you contribute and what your salary is. I worked for one employer that would match 50 percent of my contributions up to 4 percent of my salary. It was a good deal until I went to another employer that would match 100 percent of my contributions up to 5 percent of my salary. At the second employer, I was making $75k per year, and if I saved $3,750, they would give me $3,750. That was like an instant pay raise. When I was making $75k per year, it also was much easier to max out my retirement savings. The great thing was that employer contributions don't count against your 401(k) limit. So, for two years, I maxed out my 401(k) and got an extra $3,750 added to it each year.

If you are offered an employer match, you should save at least enough in your 401(k) to get all of your employer match. That's free money and is easy to get. Sometimes, the employer match is on a **vesting schedule**, which means that money is not 100 percent yours until you've stayed with the company long enough to become **vested**. As an example, the first year you may not be vested at all; year two you are 20 percent vested; year 3, 50 percent; and year 4 and beyond you could be 100 percent vested. This means that if you leave the company, you will receive only 20 percent of the company match starting in the second year, 50 percent of the match in the third year, and would get all of it in the final year.

When you leave the company, you have a few options for what you can do with your 401(k). Many 401(k) providers require that you move the money elsewhere if it is below their minimum account value. If you don't have enough in the account, you can choose to do a **rollover**, which just means to move the money to another similar retirement account. You can rollover the money to a new employer that has a 401(k), or you can rollover the money into a traditional IRA (more on this later in this chapter) if your new employer doesn't offer a 401(k) or you don't want the money tied up until you terminate your relationship with the new employer.[84]

If you do meet the plans minimum account balance requirement, you can choose to leave your money in a 401(k) there and just open a new 401(k) account with your next employer. This happens frequently, often because people don't know that they can or should move their money. I had a couple of 401(k) accounts from previous employers open that I finally consolidated[85] after I quit working for other people. For a time, it was easy to just leave them where they were at and ignore them, but I kept track of the accounts and made sure I kept my information up-to-date with the companies holding them. I believe it is important to remember where your money is, as many people forget.

Lastly, you can choose to have your 401(k) funds distributed to you when you leave employment. You then must pay taxes on the money as you would normal income, and there is often a tax penalty also due to the IRS. I strongly discourage this option unless you desperately need the money and qualify under the IRS' hardship guidelines (such as a disability).

Traditional and Roth IRAs

If you work for an employer that doesn't offer a 401(k), you are ineligible for the 401(k), or you are self-employed, you can still save for retirement using two other accounts that have tax advantages. Individual retirement accounts (IRAs) currently allow you to contribute up to $6,000 ($7,000 if you are over 50). While you can't contribute nearly as much to an IRA that you can to a 401(k), if it is your only option, it is still a good deal.

Additionally, you may choose to contribute enough to only a 401(k) to max out your employer match and then contribute to an IRA. You'll need to talk to a qualified tax consultant[86] or financial planner[87] to fully understand

---

[84] Most of the time, money in a 401(k) can't be switched between plans once it is in a plan provided by your current employer. The money can be moved or rolled over only once you leave your employer.

[85] *Consolidate,* in this instance, means to combine multiple accounts into one.

what you can and can't do when it comes to mixing and matching retirement accounts.

IRAs come in two forms: **Traditional and Roth.**

A traditional IRA allows you a tax deduction now for your contributions, similar to investing with pre-tax money in a 401(k). Your investments grow tax deferred, and when you start withdrawing money, it is taxed at your regular income rate at that time. This is a good account to utilize if you have a lot of income now and think that once you reach retirement age you will be in a lower tax bracket. It also allows you to invest more money right now because Uncle Sam isn't getting his share until later.

A Roth IRA requires that you contribute with after-tax money. When you reach retirement and start withdrawing money, any gains you've made over the years are tax free. Roth IRAs are a good tool to use if you expect your income to increase in retirement or think that there may be adjustments to tax brackets that may result in you having to pay more taxes at the time you withdrawal the money.

Which is the right option?

It depends on your situation and what you think the future will hold for you. I have both accounts. I started a Roth IRA when I was making $15k a year part time and put in about $500 a year for five years. With the benefit of ten years' time, that investment has more than tripled. While it's not enough to fund even one year of living expenses, when I take that money out, I won't have to pay taxes on it.

I also have a traditional IRA that I rolled over money from a 401(k) into, and I have contributed to after I left a job but was still making good money. This account has much more in it than my IRA just because of the 401(k) rollover.

---

[86] Often, an accountant fulfills the role of a tax consultant and tax planner.
[87] A financial planner is a person that specializes in helping people with retirement planning and determining where to put their money. They can also sell life insurance and other products.

Choosing Investments in Your Retirement Accounts

What you invest in inside of your retirement account is a complex question. I won't tell you what you should invest in, but I can tell you a bit about the basics of your options available and what I have personally done. Keep in mind that you should seek competent advice from a professional before making any investment decision.

Investing money through a retirement account immediately gives you access to investing into more than just a savings account. If you do it right, you will hopefully grow your money much more quickly than if you do it with a savings account. If you do it wrong, you could lose all your savings. No pressure!

When most people start thinking about investing, they think about buying stocks and bonds. A **stock** is a very small fractional ownership in a publicly traded company.[88] When you own stocks, you can benefit if the value of the company increases. But the company can also go down in value, and the value of your investment will go down as well. Another benefit to owning stocks is that some pay dividends. A **dividend** is a percentage of the profit that the company makes that is shared with investors like you.

A **bond** is debt that has been issued by public companies or, in some cases, by various levels of government from your local city to a county, a state, or even the national government.

When you own a stock, you are one of the owners of that company. When you own a bond, that company owes you your money back plus interest, just as you would owe the bank if you took out a loan. With a bond, you and several other people are lending companies money. Bonds are seen as less risky than stock, because in the event the company goes bankrupt, their remaining assets will first be divvied up among debt holders before anything is paid to the owners or stockholders. Bonds generally have regular payments that are made to the bond holders and a maturity date when the rest of the bond is due to be paid back.

With stock, the company is not obligated to pay off your original investment. They may or may not pay you dividends, which are a share of the

---

[88] A publicly traded company is usually a large company like McDonald's or Microsoft that has gone through the process of selling part of the company to the public in an effort to raise money at one point or to allow their original investors to more easily sell their ownership and get some money and profit back.

profits that the company makes.[89] Some companies do not pay dividends at all. These companies generally have stocks that are consider growth stocks. Investors make money on these stocks because they are going up in value significantly enough that investors can buy them and hold them until they can sell them for a good profit.

The risk with stocks is that they may decline in value or stop paying dividends. Also, the company may go bankrupt, and your entire investment could be wiped out.

If stocks are so risky, then why do people invest in them? Stocks can generate much higher returns than bonds.

So, how do you pick good investments? That's not the focus of this chapter and not something I am enough of an expert on to be comfortable telling you what to do or how to do it.

If you are like me and don't have the time to become an expert on the stock market, there are several tools you can use to invest in the stock market without having to do research on hundreds of stocks yourself.

A long-held belief is that diversification is a key component to investing. **Diversification** is when your investments are spread out over many companies and possible different asset types as well. If you were to invest your life savings in XYZ corporation and it went bankrupt tomorrow, you would lose everything. If you invest your life savings equally between XYZ corporation and ABC company, and XYZ fails but ABC doubles, then you would still have the same amount of money as you started with. This is basic diversification.

Luckily, there are several ways for you to achieve diversification and earn a good rate of return without spending months studying the stock market. The first option are mutual funds. A **mutual fund** is when a group of investors can pool their money to buy a group of stocks. Mutual funds allow you to get exposed to investments that have larger price tags (such as bonds that often require $100k to be purchased). All investors share the risks and rewards in proportion to their investment in the mutual fund.

Mutual funds make their money by charging fees based on the assets being managed. Essentially if you are receiving a 9 percent return on your money invested in a mutual fund, the fund is probably earning 10 percent or

---

[89] A company may not be able to pay dividends if it is unprofitable. It may choose to withhold dividends if it is expecting to make large investments in the future, or it may never pay dividends as part of their strategy.

more and taking their fees first. If a mutual fund loses money, they still have the right to their fees, so a loss in a mutual fund may be amplified by the fact that they still are charging you to keep your money in it.

Similar to mutual funds are ETFs or exchange-traded funds. A mutual fund is managed by a fund manager and his team of professionals with a lot of input from computer analysis. An **ETF** uses a set of rules to automatically invest into stocks or bonds based on the parameters that were set up at the start of the ETF. ETFs have a fee basis lower than that of mutual funds, and they are successful at removing the emotional elements that plague humans such as FOMO.[90]

A mutual fund or an ETF can have either a very broad or narrow focus. For a time, I held a gold ETF that invested in gold only. I also invested into one that tracked the Dow Jones Industrial Average,[91] so it proportionally held all the companies that were listed there. There are also mutual funds that do the same thing. You can invest in either mutual funds or ETFs that focus on tech stocks, manufacturing stocks, large-cap or small-cap stocks,[92] and more. When making my own investments, I have preferred to invest in ETFs over mutual funds, because they generally have a lower-fee structure.

One of my favorite tools to invest in is a **target-date retirement fund**, sometimes referred to as an age-based fund. A target-date fund is usually a mutual fund that is meant to simplify the investing process. It has long been believed that you should be invested more heavily in stocks when you are young in order to maximize the gain potential from them while you have time on your side to overcome any potential market downturns. As you age, the common advice states that you should move more to bonds, which provide steady income. Target-date funds are designed to do this automatically for you.

Target-date funds are a favorite tool of company-sponsored 401(k) plans. It is easy for an employee to determine when they wish to retire and pick a plan with a target date that is in line with their retirement date.

---

[90] Fear of missing out.

[91] The DJIA is a common measurement of the health of the stock market, but it really tracks the performance of only thirty large companies listed on stock exchanges in the U.S.

[92] A large-cap stock is when the total value of all the company shares being traded on the stock exchange is more than $5 billion (e.g., Microsoft). A small-cap stock is when the total value of all the company shares being traded on the stock exchange is between $300 million and $2 billion.

Untraditional Investments

By now you know that I am a big proponent of real estate as a tool to build wealth and passive income. Both of them can help provide for you in retirement. If you have the risk tolerance, then real estate may be a good option for you to invest in as well. But it is not the only other option out there.

Another passive income investment is to buy or create loans (commonly referred to as notes). If you have the money, you can choose to buy notes from people, companies, or even banks. You can buy performing notes, meaning that owed money is paid regularly. Or you can buy non-performing notes, meaning the people have stopped making payments. In either case, I recommend that you seek a ton of additional education on the subject, because some notes are unsecured, and you could be buying a note that will soon be wiped out by bankruptcy. Conversely, if you buy a note secured by real estate, you can foreclose on the home and have a new home you can either sell or rent out.

You can also choose to act as a lender and make loans to others. It is a very common practice among real estate investors to obtain private financing such as yours. I have also seen people successfully lend money on cars or business equipment. Be careful about making loans on your own, as there are a lot of rules and regulations that go into it. That's why I would prefer someone else to make the loan so that I can just buy it from them.[93]

If owning a small fraction of a giant company doesn't appeal to you because you can't help that company's performance, you could invest in a smaller company directly. Have you always wanted to start your own business? Or do you know someone starting a business, who needs you to be an investor? Either way, you could have a direct impact on a business in your local community. You can help bring customers in and make money. When you are tired of the business, you can then sell it for a multiple of the profit. Common multiples lie between three and five times earnings (profit). So, you could have a business making you $100k a year for ten years and then sell it when you retire for $500k.

Where do you find the money to buy a rental property, mortgage note, or business? The easiest way is to buy them with cash, but not everyone has cash sitting around. However, if you've built up your other retirement accounts,

---

[93] I still verify that they made the loan correctly, but it takes a lot of stress off me.

you have some options to use those funds to invest in some of these alternative assets.

Other than paying a tax penalty for withdrawing money from your retirement accounts, there are two primary options available to you to use retirement money: a **ROBS plan** and a **Self-Directed IRA**. A Self-Directed IRA allows you to use your retirement money to buy real estate, notes, and ownership in a business. Due to IRS rules, owning a business in a Self-Directed IRA prohibits the owner from earning a salary from the business or being allowed to personally guarantee (see chapter 7) any loan taken out by the business. A Self-Directed IRA requires you to roll your retirement account over to a company that specializes in these types of plans. Not all Self-Directed IRA companies are equal. Some advertise as self-directed, but they simply allow you to invest in more stock market transactions and don't really let you invest in alternative assets.

A ROBS Plan stands for Rollover for Business Startups and is designed specifically to allow you to use your retirement funds to purchase a business that you are going to work in and lets you guarantee any loan for the business. There are companies that specialize in these types of plans and can walk you through opening one up, as there are multiple steps.

If businesses and real estate aren't your thing or are outside of your price range, than maybe you can use your creative side to make money. If you are a creative person, a way to earn passive income is through the development of **intellectual property (IP)**. Intellectual property is things like books, songs, or inventions.[94] I like to lump in your social media pages and blogs here as well. Books, songs and inventions can earn you ongoing royalty revenue. Royalties are like someone paying you rent for the use of your patent or playing your song on the radio. With a book, you may receive royalties from a publisher who has the sole right to produce and sell the book, or they may pay you just a percentage of the profits from every book sold.

An Instagram page, a blog, a YouTube channel, or any other online presence that you build a following around can earn you additional revenue. Or other companies may pay you to promote their items in your feed. Some people build followings based around things rather than themselves with the intent that they can sell the page to a company. For instance, a page with a variety of makeup tips could be sold to a cosmetics company.

---

[94] Inventions should be *patented*, which means the government recognizes you as the inventor. This also gives you the sole right to produce the item for a period.

Intellectual property and social media followings can be more labor intensive to create or build but are often less expensive to start and grow than a regular brick and mortar business.

Why I Want My Daughter to Know This

Kids don't get it. I didn't get it until I was out of college, had a wife, a daughter, and a mortgage, and no extra money. My father had tried to tell me when I started working at sixteen that I should save some of the money for retirement one day. I remember the conversation, and I know I didn't do anything about it. Even if I had wanted to, I wouldn't have known where to start.

As an adult, I managed my own investments until I felt I had enough to have a financial planner be interested in talking to me. I waited for too long. I could have been (1) earning better rates on my money I had in savings accounts and (2) having more stable growth in my retirement accounts.

I also didn't invest enough early enough. I should have opened a retirement account as early as possible and put money into it. Back in high school, I worked as a server for a while and often just cashed my paycheck and put a little into savings. I had a few thousand dollars in one-dollar bills just sitting in my room—not even in a savings account where I could have earned some minimal interest!

If you know there are options out there waiting for you to take advantage of them, then you will be able to ask good questions at a much earlier point in your life and maximize your lifetime savings growth.

17: MONEY AND KIDS

"I want to order off the big menu!" Ashla proclaimed when she was about six years old.

My wife and I exchanged sidelong glances. We figured this day had been coming. The kid was eating everything put in front of her as she went through her latest growth spurt. The $4 kids' menu just wasn't cutting it anymore.

"Okay," I agreed to hesitantly. "They have bigger burgers that you can have and larger chicken tenders."

"No," she said bluntly and began looking at all the colorful pictures. After a few minutes, she jabbed her finger down on a page, "I want that!"

"What is it?" my wife asked setting aside her menu.

"It's lobster and steak!"

Having your own kids is a big financial commitment. Raising a child to the age of eighteen can cost nearly $250,000, without factoring in college tuition.[95] The good thing is that you don't have to spend all the money up front. But that is still a staggering amount of money to consider, which is why many people wait to have children until they are in a better financial situation.

For many people, just having a baby is an expensive process. Due to infertility, many couples are forced to seek alternatives such as fertility treatments,[96] surrogates,[97] or adoption, which all cost money. The costs on these can vary so much with insurance, the source of the surrogate, or where and how you choose to adopt that I can't even begin to place a dollar amount on it.

At the other end of the spectrum, some people get pregnant before they

---

[95] https://www.usatoday.com/story/money/personalfinance/2018/02/26/raising-child-costs-233-610-you-financially-prepared-parent/357243002/.
[96] Medical treatments requiring frequent doctor visits and hormone medication.
[97] Utilizing another person to get pregnant and carry your baby to term.

are ready. My family falls into this category. My wife and I were newlyweds but still in college, and both of us were still working part-time jobs typical of college students. We were not financially ready to have a child, but it's been great, and I wouldn't trade the experience for anything.

Since we were not in a good financial position when Ashla was born, it was a scary time for us. Luckily, my mother was able to retire and step in to help babysit. Alternatively, one of us would have been forced to drop out of college. One of the biggest financial hurdles with having a child is that someone has to be present to take care of it. We were used to both of us being able to work and go to school at the same time. I cut back my work schedule considerably, while Rebecca kept working, and we took out student loans in order to finish college.

Our school schedule required frequent baby swaps on campus so the other person could go to class. Then my mother would watch Ashla from Thursday through Sunday, which allowed us to have some overlap in classes and to cram in as many work hours as possible. As a couple, my wife and I rarely saw each other, and we would go weeks without spending more than a few minutes in each other's company. We joked that the only time we spent together were the five hours we were both sleeping.

It was hard, and after we got through it, we found out that there were programs that could have helped us immensely.

WIC (Women, Infants, Children) is a federally funded program and is part of **SNAP (food stamps)**.[98] It helps pay for healthcare and nutrition for expectant mothers and their children up to the age of five.

Head Start is another federal program that helps children in low-income homes. From birth to the age of five, kids can attend programs in schools and childcare centers. It helps ensure that kids are ready for school and receive basic health screenings. Head Start also assists with family well-being by helping parents achieve financial stability.

Both programs would have been of immense support to us. The healthcare aspect of WIC would have removed a large financial burden on us in the form of the health insurance we were carrying on Rebecca and eventually Ashla. The nutritional support would have cut down on our food bills. Head start would have allowed both us to work a lot more and achieve financial strength much earlier.

I wish I'd known because the help would have been appreciated. While I

---

[98] SNAP stands for Supplemental Nutrition Assistance Program.

think the struggle made us stronger, I want you to be aware of these options in case you don't have the support from family and friends that we had.

Once you start having kids, it is often easier and cheaper to have a second kid close in time to having the first. Having a second child just a few years after the first allows you to make use of hand-me-down clothes and toys. You can also re-use the same crib and changing table. It becomes more economical to buy in bulk. Some daycares, preschools, and private schools offer a sibling discount for the second child so that it is not that same cost repeated a second time. If your children can share a room and bathroom, then your housing costs can remain the same.

If you determine your kids can't share a room and you must move, your housing costs may go up if you have another child. Same thing with your car. Your sedan may fit you, your spouse, and the first two kids just fine. But add a third and suddenly you need a minivan or a large SUV. If you have your kids too close together, then you need multiple cribs, multiple car seats, and other stuff, and suddenly you aren't saving any money on the second child.

Why I Want My Daughter to Know This

The week after my daughter was born, both my wife and I were back to work. She may have qualified to take time off under the *Family Medical Leave Act*, because she had taken a manager promotion and was a full-time employee, but we didn't have enough money for her to be out of work for more than a few days.

The second Thursday after Ashla was born, I was getting ready for my evening shift at the ice cream store. Ashla was asleep in the other room. Rebecca came home from school (the Spring semester started two days after Ashla had been born) and began changing.

"I'll see you at about eight tonight," I said to her as I pulled on my shirt.

"No, more like eleven," she replied.

"No, it's not a closing shift," I fired right back.

"I know."

"We close at ten; the shift goes to only 7:30," I stated.

It dawned on us that we were both scheduled to work at the same time, and we had no one to watch Ashla. In the space of a few minutes, one of our good friends agreed to watch Ashla for a few hours so we could both work.

After that debacle, we got really good about scheduling (in the days before we had a shared Google calendar). That incident was a defining moment for us. We realized we couldn't both work and earn money like we had been. We were living well for a couple of college kids. We had bought a house before Rebecca got pregnant. Having used up all scholarships and grants, we had been able to pay for the remainder of our college costs in cash up until that point.

It got really hard for the next couple of years until we both finished college. Unnecessarily hard, because we didn't know about Head Start or WIC (and I am sure there are other programs we could have tapped into also).

I want my daughter to know this so she knows to ask the right questions and seek help if she has a child before she is ready. Hopefully, she can wait and have kids a bit later when she and her significant other decide they are ready. I hope the information here can help her determine whether she is.

18: WHEN THE WORST HAPPENS

"Dad, have you ever had money problems?"

"I missed a few payments when I was younger. This was right when automatic payment was becoming a big thing, and I didn't have it yet. I've also maxed out my credit cards a couple of times and even had an overage fee."

"They let you go over your limit?"

"Yeah, they liked the $35 they charged me for it too."

"But have you ever had any real money problems?"

"Not really. Your mother and I both are very diligent with our money. Spending time as a payday lender, a tax preparer, and a banker made me very aware of people's spending habits. I once had a customer as a payday lender that was making $80,000 a year. He was married with two kids, and they rented a small house. At the time, your mother and I made a combined $55,000 a year. We owned our own home and two rentals. The guy drove a nice truck and showed up with Starbucks. I rode my bike and didn't drink much coffee. Living on less than we spent has kept us from money problems."

Sometimes, all the planning, budgeting, saving, and insuring isn't enough. Job loss, disability, and death can affect anyone at just about any time. They all have major financial repercussions in your life. Furthermore, some poor financial decisions on your part or that of your partner can also lead to financial hardship.

I hope that you never have to deal with any of the following things but you should know the basics of what each is in case you have to face it. What follows are common situations that people find themselves in when they struggle with money continuously or if they just hit a rough patch in life.

A **Repossession** is when you fail to make payments on a car (or sometimes an appliance or other high-value item that you've financed), and the company that financed takes it back. They are hoping they can re-sell the item to recoup some of the losses they incurred when you stopped making payments.

A **Collection** stems from an unpaid bill. As a banker, I saw a lot of people with collections stemming from unpaid medical bills. When you owe money to someone, whether it is a bank or a cell phone company, and you stop paying them, you are still legally responsible to pay that money. The company will try to get you to pay for a time, and if you don't, they will sell your collection account to another company. This gets the original company a small fraction of what you owe, and it is up to the other company to try to collect the full amount from you. Because they paid only a fraction of the amount you owe, they may be willing to settle for a lesser amount. They win because they've made money and you win because you don't owe the whole thing.

Often, your collection account will keep being sold from company to company if you are still unable to pay. Collections can typically continue for anywhere from four to six years. However, this period restarts with every payment you make. It can also be refreshed if you acknowledge to the company that you owe the debt. Be careful when talking to the collection companies, as you may just be encouraging them to harass you longer. Often, the collection will fall off your credit report after seven years (unless it was satisfied before then), but the collection companies can keep calling you.

A **Judgment** takes the collection process up a notch. Judgments are usually used with only larger amounts, because it involves taking you to court[99] and having the court issue a legal finding against you. The judgment then allows the debt collector to use garnishment (when they contact your employer, and your employer has to legal pay them a portion of your wages[100]) . A judgment can also lead to a lien placed on any piece of real estate you own (such as your home) and sometimes against other assets. A lien is like a mortgage in that when you sell the property the judgment lien has to be paid off prior to the home transferring to another person.

We somewhat discussed an **eviction** in chapter 13, but an eviction occurs when you are renting a place to live and fail to pay the rent. Rarely, an eviction can also occur for violating other terms of the lease, such as noise or odor covenants.[101] An eviction follows a process when you will be served

---

[99] Not showing up to your court date usually means you aren't contesting the debt, and the judgment is almost always granted.
[100] Wages is income you earn from your job.
[101] A covenant is a fancy word for a term or a condition in the lease.

notice, have a court date, and then physically be moved out of the place by the landlord. Each state is different. In some states, the eviction process can be as short as three days. In other states, it can take as long as nine months. Unlike other items in this list, an eviction doesn't necessarily show up on your credit report, but it will show up in most background checks.

If you own your home and stop paying the monthly mortgage, then a **foreclosure**[102] is started. The foreclosure process is when the bank takes the property from you for not paying. Since it is your home, it can be a long process. The bank really wants you to catch up on your payments and may be willing to work with you to achieve this. They may be able to defer some payments, when they move the past due payments to the end of the loan. They may be able to give you resources such as debt counselors to help you budget. At the end of the day, if you don't pay, the bank will take your home and sell it to recoup their money. Before that happens, you should try to sell it yourself so that your credit isn't damaged further and to hopefully get back any equity that you have built up. This is discussed in more detail later in this chapter.

Bankruptcy is the end of the line. If you have done everything you can to repay money you've borrowed and you can't, bankruptcy may be your best option. There are two primary types of bankruptcy. A chapter 7 bankruptcy is when you allow the court to sell your assets (house, car, and other valuables) to pay back what is owed. Unsecured debt like credit cards and medical debt typically do not end up getting repaid but are wiped clean, and you no longer have to repay them.

A chapter 13 bankruptcy requires you to develop a budget and restructure your payments on terms you can afford. You pay the court, and the court makes your new loan payments for you, based on your plan. This may stretch your payments out over a longer period but brings down the monthly payments to a manageable level.

There are other types of bankruptcy as well, but they are mostly for businesses and farmers. It is important to note that you can just file bankruptcy to discharge medical debt. Many people who are uninsured or underinsured[103] have had to use this option when insurance didn't cover the

---

[102] Foreclosure is a term for the process, not the end result. Many people think of a foreclosed home as one the bank has taken back, but that is technically a REO (Real Estate Owned).

[103] *Underinsured* means that you have less insurance than is required by the bank.

cost of an emergency.

These events are all likely to impact your credit score negatively. Bankruptcy can stay on your credit report for seven–ten years, depending on the type you file. A foreclosure also stays on your credit report for seven years. Collections, repossessions, and judgments stay on your credit report for various amounts of time. The impact from all of these can be felt for years. It is very difficult to obtain financing right after a bankruptcy and is likely to be very expensive (high interest).

Ideally, you should make all your payments on time. But if you can't, then you should be aware of your options. All debt collectors must follow rules laid down by the *Fair Debt Collection Practices Act*. This means they can't call you after a certain time at night or before a certain time in the morning. They can't threaten you, and if you declare bankruptcy, they must cease all collection practices against you once they've received notification.

If you find yourself in a situation when you can't pay, don't hide from it. Many times you have options if you just answer the phone when the bank calls. They may be able to restructure your payments or refer you to someone that can help you. You will never know these things if you hide from it. You should also seek information about your situation. Google is an anonymous way to find information, but you may also want to talk to a debt counselor or a bankruptcy lawyer to understand all of your options.

What Happens If I Can't Make My Mortgage Payment?

There may be a time when you have everything under control only to see it all slip away. Whatever the cause may be, you should be prepared for what happens if you can no longer make your mortgage payment.

Once you've missed your first payment, the bank will try to get in contact with you to remind you to pay. This may be by letter, phone call, email, or all of the above. The bank wants you to make the payment; they do not want to proceed any further.

If you still don't pay, the bank will start the foreclosure process. This is when the bank proceeds with court filing against you in an effort to take possession of the home. Foreclosure is not as quick as an eviction, but the

---

If you have a home that would cost $200,000 to rebuild and you have only $150,000 of insurance on it, then you are underinsured by $50,000. If it burns down, you have to come up with $50,000 plus your deductible to get it rebuilt.

laws regarding it vary from state to state. In all likelihood, you will not be kicked out of your home for several months, and the bank will try to work with you to get you caught up and halt the foreclosure.

The worst thing you can do is pretend like nothing is wrong and hide from the bank. Without talking to you, the bank has to assume the worst and proceed with a foreclosure as quickly as possible.

If you respond to phone calls and letters, the bank may have options available to you to keep you in your home. This can include a one-time payment deferral when your missed loan payment(s) is moved to the tail end of the loan, and you start fresh with the next payment due. The bank may also be able to put you on a modified payment schedule to make up the missed payment(s) over the next several months. They may refer you to a debt counselor that has more options available to you, or they may have other options unique to your situation.

You should be proactive and try to sell your home if you know you won't be able to make payments going forward. This will get the bank paid off, keep a foreclosure off your credit report, and may result in some cash in your pocket if there is money left over from the sale of your home after paying off the bank.

Foreclosure is not a fun process, but you can't hide from it. Don't be so ashamed that you refuse to seek help.

I once saw a gentleman lose his home after he had lost his job. He stopped making payments on his second mortgage (my bank held the first). He would talk to me about what was going on because he still had his payments with me current. I encouraged him to talk to a debt counselor. I also knew he had equity in the home—enough to pay off both loans and walk away with about $20k after selling costs. I told him he should try to sell it, but he didn't want to talk to a real estate agent. When it was all done, the second mortgage took possession of the property and paid off the loan my bank had. Then they sold the property and used the $20k to pay their attorney costs and kept the rest.

Why I Want My Daughter to Know This

I don't want my daughter to ever be faced with any of these situations, but there are many things outside of her control. By learning about these things, she can regain control of the situation and avoid becoming a victim.

As a lender, I couldn't help people if they wouldn't pick up the phone and help themselves. Multiple times I had options available to restructure payments for people, but they refused to talk to me and instead lost their home or business.

Further, many people are too proud to accept help. I knew other people that could have brought payments current with a call to their parents or relatives. They could have sold their home instead of losing it. If they had a good business and just experienced a rough patch, they could have brought in an investor and given up part of the company but kept the business running.

If you can't make payments don't be too proud to accept help.

On the back end of things, don't be ashamed afterwards. Life moves on, and you should too. Reflect on what happened and try to determine what mistakes you made. A victim of a bad economy is still at fault for not having enough savings. Recognize your faults and correct them. Don't let it happen again. Bad situations are a lesson, and if you repeat the same mistake a second time, then you can feel ashamed.

19: SPOTTING A SCAM AND AVOIDING IDENTITY THEFT

"My computer has a virus?" I repeated back to the person on the other end of the phone as Ashla and I were sitting in my office. She was doing her school work, and I was interrupted while paying the bills.

The voice on the other end of the phone confirmed it in a thick accent.

"I don't have a computer," I lied. "How can it have a virus?"

Ashla looked up from what she was doing and stared at me questioningly. The man on the other end of the phone continued to tell me my computer had a virus and they needed to download something in order to remove the virus.

"Oh, it sounds serious," I mocked. "I'd better go buy a computer so you can remove the virus."

The man said they needed to do it right away.

"Well, it's going to take me a couple hours to go buy a computer, so I have a computer, so it can get infected by a virus, so you can remove the virus."

The man got upset. He stated they needed to remove the virus now.

"But I don't have the computer yet!" I protested.

The man finally got it and asked what I meant. I repeated that I didn't have a computer. He said they were sure I did.

"Well I don't," I stated firmly. "And even if I did, I wouldn't give some scumbag access to it so they can steal my stuff." I used a few colorful words to describe his mating habits and then hung up.

"Who was that?" Ashla asked.

"Just another scammer," I replied turning back to what I was doing.

"How do you know?" she asked.

"Microsoft won't ever call you about a virus. That's not what they do. I have antivirus software for that, and they don't call either. If someone you don't know calls you and tells you something terrible has happened, they are trying to prey on your emotions."

"So, why didn't you just hang up?" she asked. She's seen me hang up on scammers

dozens of times before.

"There was a live person on the other end this time. If he's going to waste my time I thought I'd at least have some fun with it and waste his time too."

As hard as you work to keep your money, there will be people working just as hard to con you out of your money. If a criminal can't get your money, they may settle for stealing your identity so that they can steal money from banks and credit card companies.

Identity Theft

Identity theft occurs when someone takes your personal information, such as your name, social security number, address, etc., and uses it without your permission. Criminals can use your identity to open credit cards or take out loans in your name. They get money from lenders and never repay it, which damages your credit.

If they get your insurance information, they can use it to file claims and get money from insurance companies for damage to your stuff that never occurred. As sad as it is, sometimes they use your medical insurance in order to receive treatment because they can't afford insurance on their own.

You may find it shocking that you have lost points from your driver's license for traffic tickets that you never got. Some criminals drive using another person's license. It can even be taken a step further, when they commit crimes and serve jail time in your name. It's fun when you apply for a job only to be turned down because they think you served jail time.

Tax time has become a favorite time of year for criminals. They discovered they can file a tax return on your behalf and receive your refund. Sometimes, people will work under your identity all year long. At the end of the year, they may not even file taxes; however, their employer has been reporting wages to the government under your social security number. This could cause you to be audited[104] for under-reporting your income.

There are dozens more ways that criminals can use your identity for their own gain. Back in chapter 15, I touched on identity theft and the insurance you can obtain to help protect yourself. Identity theft insurance helps you

---

[104] An audit is an investigation by the IRS into the tax returns you have filed. An audit requires you to provide the proof (paperwork) to back up whatever is on your tax return.

clean up the mess that criminals make of your credit. It also usually provides monitoring of your credit report. That way, you know whether anyone is trying to open up accounts in your name.

If you don't have insurance and your identity gets stolen, there are some basic things you can do to get started on fixing things. First would be to file a police report. You may need this to present to companies to prove that there was a malicious act by someone besides you. You then want to put a freeze on your credit. You need to contact one of the credit bureaus (Experian, Equifax, or TransUnion) to do this. A credit freeze lasts for seven years, and sometimes can last longer. It prevents anyone from pulling your credit.[105]

The credit bureau will allow you to have access to your credit report so you can see what has occurred. You have to review your credit report and then inform the credit bureau of fraudulent items. Sometimes, the credit bureau can clean them up for you; other times, you will have to reach out to the companies themselves to get them removed. The credit bureau also allows you to input comments on items on your report. So, if you are disputing something, you can leave a note on your credit for anyone to see when you have your credit checked for your own loan purposes (see chapter 6 for more on credit).

Scams

Beware of "too good to be true" offers. A free vacation, a Nigerian prince, or a rich dead uncle you didn't know you had are just a few of the ways that scammers attempt to turn your money into their money.

Scammers use a variety of platforms to reach you. Phone, email, social media, and even snail mail are all unsafe. Typically, scammers try to elicit an emotional reaction from you. Those claiming to be from the IRS prey on your fear. They threaten you with jail if you don't pay immediately. A Nigerian prince offers you money to get at your greed. A stranded traveler tugs at your heartstrings.

Scams usually start when a scammer gets a couple of pieces of your information and attempts to persuade you to give them money or trick you into revealing enough about yourself that they can steal your identity. Once they identify a person, phone number, or email, they begin trying to contact

---

[105] This is a pain when you want to take out a new loan, because you have to coordinate with the lender and the credit bureau. It is worth it though.

you.

The easiest way to avoid scams is not to give out your information to someone that calls you out of the blue. The IRS will never call you. A lawyer representing a rich dead estranged relative is highly unlikely to call you but will support their position with proof. The Social Security Administration won't call you, threatening to cut off your benefits.

Nobody will accept payment by asking you to buy gift cards and tell them the numbers on the back.

More insidious are scams done in person. These often occur with someone selling you something. While you do receive the product, it isn't anything like you expected. I've been scammed twice. I once bought a magazine subscription from a person going door to door, telling the story of their kid and how they were trying to get their life back on track. The guy may have been honest, but the company behind him was not. I got conned out of $70 here.

The other scam involved buying an investment property. It involved a real estate conference my partner attended and a property sold to them at that time. They got us for $17,000.

At the end of the day, you have to verify what people are telling and selling you. I should have checked out the company that sold me the magazine subscription as well as the company that sold my partner and me the investment property. A search through the Better Business Bureau[106] would have revealed a lot of upset former customers for both companies. Unfortunately, good judgment comes from experience, and experience comes from making bad decisions.

Protecting Your Information

Rather than having to deal with the aftermath of identity theft or suffering from a scam, it is best to avoid them and protect yourself in the first place. The old adage of "an ounce of prevention is worth a pound of cure" still holds true. You will feel out of control and somewhat helpless if you fall victim to one of these criminals, so it's better to exercise control in the first place.

When I was in banking, we were trained continuously on how to protect

---

[106] Find the Better Business Bureau (BBB) online. They allow you submit complaints and sometimes help facilitate resolving them.

financial information. Once a year, we would have an annual in-person training when we discussed privacy protection. Then, we would get online video trainings at least twice more each year. Then, to make sure that we were being diligent in our practices, they would test us throughout the year when we were least expecting it. The results of the tests would determine whether we would attend additional trainings. Then, the results of the tests would be discussed with us at management meetings. We got pretty good about spotting fake emails and suspicious activity.

Getting your information is the first hurdle for criminals and can be done in person, over the phone, or electronically. To get your information in person, a criminal can approach you and start asking you questions, but this is very unlikely. More likely is that a criminal will either attempt to steal your information from you or go dumpster diving. Dumpster diving is exactly what it sounds like; this tactic means a criminal goes through your trash to find documents that should have been shredded.

As a rule, you should shred any document that has sensitive information. Bank/credit card statements, cancelled checks (if you use checks), and any piece of paper you may have written a password on—all fall into this category. I like to shred my utility bills as well, but that's probably me just being paranoid.

Another way that criminals can steal information in person is via shoulder surfing. This is when they simply look over your shoulder as you log in to your bank account at a coffee shop or other public place. This can occur in a more private location such as your home or workplace as well but is less common.

Always be aware of your surroundings when checking sensitive information online. If your creepy coworker is hanging out right behind you, then you may want to wait for a better time.

If you are like me, then you probably leave documents spread across your workspace. This is the way I think. I need to see the projects I am working on, and it helps me organize my thoughts. I can look over my workspace to get a feel for what I need to prioritize. I can get away with this at home because no one goes into my office except for me. As a banker, I had two options: (1) put everything in a locked cabinet at night, or (2) lock the door to my office when I left for the day. After locking my keys in my office one day, I decided to keep everything locked in the cabinet.

It doesn't take long for a thief to swipe a piece of paper or just snap a picture with their cell phone. The same can be said of information pulled up on your computer. Outside of your home, you should make a habit of locking your computer any time you step away from it. You don't want anyone sitting down to look through your email or potentially plugging in a thumb drive with a virus or keystroke logger,[107] which brings us to how criminals steal information electronically. Without proper virus protection, you can be exposed to a denial-of-service attack,[108] keystroke logger, or other malware that can either destroy your computer or steal your sensitive information. You should always have good antivirus software, but using good judgment is better. Don't visit suspicious websites,[109] and don't click on suspicious links.

A common attack via email is called phishing. It requires that you click a link in the email, which allows a virus to be downloaded to your computer. These emails look official and are designed to mimic what you would expect from a bank or online retailer (such as Amazon). Read the email address to see whether it looks legitimate. If it does, but you are still suspicious, you can hover your mouse over the link to see what website path it will display. If you are still uncertain, open your browser and go to the website without clicking anything in the email. You can log in to your account that way and see whether there are any messages for you.

Email also opens the door to scams such as the Nigerian prince.[110] Such emails are sent out randomly to massive email lists compiled by criminals. These scams require you to respond to the email. The scammer will then try to lure you into sending them money or gift cards. Sometimes, they will send you a small check first and have you deposit it. They will then ask you to send them or another recipient a portion of it back. Once you do, their original check bounces, the bank takes back the money they "put in your account,"

---

[107] A keystroke logger makes note of what buttons you hit on your keyboard and then sends it to the criminal electronically. It is an easy way for criminals to capture usernames and passwords.

[108] A denial-of-service attack is when a criminal locks you out of your own computer and demands payment from you to release your computer back to you.

[109] I once heard that church websites are more likely to have viruses than porn websites due to a lack of capital and computer expertise at most churches, whereas porn websites are very judicious in ensuring proper virus protection and spend money on computer experts.

[110] I once read scammers keep using the Nigerian prince scam because anyone who has heard about it will ignore it. But the naïve, who are their primary targets, are the only ones likely to respond. Thus, those that respond to it are much more likely to fall for the scam.

and the scammer takes off with your money.

Be cautious when accepting checks from strangers. Criminals also target people selling stuff online. By overpaying for something and requesting you give them back the overage, they are hoping you will both turn over the item to them as well as give them some cash for their trouble.

These sorts of fraud can also be committed in person or over the phone. As I mentioned earlier, the IRS will never call you demanding immediate payment of back taxes. The Social Security Administration will not call you and threaten to suspend your benefits. That's not the way the government operates. They most certainly won't accept payment in the form of gift cards. Don't be stupid, or the criminals will win!

Why I Want My Daughter to Know This

I got so used to credit and debit cards being stolen when I was in banking that it stopped being frustrating. It happened so frequently that when it happened to me it wasn't a big deal. I new the laws in my state, which protected me from suffering losses. The laws, and even just good business practices on behalf of banks, mean that the bank will cover money charged to stolen credit/debit card, provided you let them know in a timely manner. They build a line item into their budgets for these losses.

Being exposed to these losses every day allowed me to be impressed rather than angry when my wallet was stolen. My wallet was stolen out of my car when I was attending a Turkey Trot 5k on Thanksgiving. I didn't notice until late the next day. The thief had gone Black Friday shopping. It just so happened they went to Best Buy where I had an account and registered my card. I got a detailed list of everything they bought. Since it was Black Friday, they got some great deals. For $1,300, they got really cool stuff, and I wish I had spent that money myself.

My point is that you will likely experience a stolen credit card or identity theft in your life. Take steps to prevent it as much as possible, but don't let it get under your skin at the end of the day. The criminals have already stolen your money. Don't let them steal your time and energy as well.

It is a very real possibility that with all the data breaches that continue to occur, everything a criminal needs to steal your identity with is already on the dark web[111] where identity thieves can buy information in bulk. I had all my

---

[111] The dark web are websites that don't show up in Google. They are used to do

bank documents, social security number, and more stolen from a lockbox at a mortgage brokerage. More than likely, that information is out on the web somewhere now. I never had any problems with any of those accounts nor did I have any weird inquiries on my credit, but I am aware that my personal information is no longer private.

These things happen. Protect yourself as much as you can, but don't stress about it. Buy ID theft insurance, don't click on suspicious stuff, don't buy gift cards for people at the other end of a telephone.

---

illegal things.

20: THE IMPORTANCE OF GIVING BACK

"Why do we volunteer, Dad?"

"There are so many people in the world that need help, Ashla. We may not have much, but we have more than most. We have time to prepare food boxes for those in need at the food bank, which is sometimes more important than giving money. When we were in need, others helped us out."

"I thought we didn't get food from the food bank?"

"We didn't, but we received heat help from LEAP. When our sewer line broke, our family gave us money to put towards repairs. When we needed a babysitter so we could continue to work, your grandma stepped up along with some of our friends. We've received help from so many over the years that we could never repay. So we help others."

"So why don't we volunteer more?"

I have heard from many people that anything you give you will get back at least twice over. If you give money, you will get back more money. If you give time, you will get back more time. I don't know whether that is true. I feel like it is. As I've donated money, I've been able to grow my income and net worth. When I started volunteering my time, I found that I had more time for myself.

The concept is hard to swallow, and it is difficult to give away money when you have very little. When your paycheck may not even cover all your expenses that month, it is very difficult to think about giving any of it away. It was difficult for me. I still don't believe in regular tithing,[112] whether it be to a place of worship or charity.[113]

I do like to give to those in need around me. I may go months without

---

[112] Tithing is a form of regular giving when you give a percentage of everything you earn. Places of worship encourage tithing as a way for their members to give regularly. Ten percent of income is a common amount that is given.

[113] I did try tithing 10 percent for a time, but it never felt good.

donating anything and then give away several thousand to a person or a cause I feel could make the most of it. I enjoy the feeling of making a single significant impact in someone's life or helping an organization.

For me, giving away money isn't something I have to do, but is something I want to do. I want to be able to change the world. In order for me to change the world, I have to have the money to do so. Being able to give away money encourages me to be more successful in my work and more diligent with my money. It is something that keeps me motivated.

Giving away money or time should feel good. If it doesn't feel good, are you giving to the right causes? If not, check in with your situation and why you are giving.

As a nameless member of a large church giving never felt good. No one thanked me for my monthly donation. The money came out automatically from my bank account, so I didn't really notice it was going anywhere. I never saw the difference my donation made.

When tax laws changed in 2018, reaching the threshold where it made sense to give to non-profits became much more difficult. This was one of the reasons I changed my outlook. It no longer made financial sense to find a non-profit to give to as a tax write-off. Suddenly, it became more acceptable to give directly to people in need. The rise of GoFundMe makes it easy to do so as well.

In addition to giving money, I like to give my time. I have come to realize that I get as much (or more) from volunteering as I put into it. As I mentioned in the very first chapter, volunteering helped me build my resume when I was still working for others. While I was never asked about my education in a job interview, I was asked about the volunteering activities I listed.

Volunteering has helped me build relevant business skills. As I write this, I currently sit on the board of two not-for-profit organizations. I serve as Vice-Chair for one and Treasurer for the other. Being involved with them means that I am regularly having conversations about managing budgets, hiring and firing, and planning. Additionally, it taught me about *Robert's Rules of Order*, which is how many organizations run meetings where voting and decisions take place.

Through my volunteer work, I have made several friends and acquaintances, and some of them I have even done business with. If you run your own business or you are in sales, volunteering is free networking and free advertising. If allowed, you can post your volunteer work to social media to build your own personal brand.

Give freely and give with joy. There will always be more money.

Why I Want My Daughter to Know This

Having been involved with many organizations as a volunteer, I have witnessed a steady decline in giving both of time and money. People say they don't have time, or they lack the motivation. Whatever the reason, it's sad to see people thinking that interacting on social media is the equivalent to interacting in person and see volunteerism suffer.

Volunteering is a great way to build relationships with people. It feels good and can be a lot of fun. If you've ever felt like you've nothing to do, or you are tired of spending money to do things, volunteering is a great alternative. Decide on an organization and make it a regular practice to volunteer with them. If you are interested in a board position, talk with salesmen (bankers, insurance brokers, real estate agents), as many of them are involved with boards that are looking to recruit new members.

I want my daughter to feel comfortable giving money away. I want her to get to the point of having an abundance of money and being able to do with it whatever she wants. I hope to instill in her a giving nature so that she can solve real problems in the world.

21: REAL TIPS TO SAVE MONEY

"Wow, that's expensive!" I said as I looked at the cost of two different syrups. I had been sent to the store to pick up a few things. One of them was syrup, and the sender had specifically told me that her kids would eat only one specific type of syrup.

"Not really. It's less than five dollars," my daughter replied.

"I meant in comparison to each other," I said. My wife and I typically stick with a store brand, or budget items if the health benefits are the same. We will pay more for healthier food, but when picking a syrup, we always go the cheapest route possible. "Look, this one is $1.59, and the one they want is $3.39. It's more than double."

"Do you think it adds up to much?"

"Well, not all items will be double," I theorized. "But if just half of them are, they easily are spending 50 percent more than they need to on something they are just going to poop out later."

Ashla laughed. "How much do you think they spend?"

"Well, we have a slightly smaller family and spend around $400 a month. So, they are probably spending about $600 a month. It's costing them $2,400 more per year than it needs to."

These are things my wife and I did to save money over the years:

1. Budget food shopping. From the example above, budgeting could save you $200/month or $2,400 a year.
2. Drink tap water when eating out. Two adults not getting a soda each for $1.99 with their meal while eating out twice a week can save $206.96 per year. Water is better for you anyway. Avoid alcohol at restaurants. One beer each at $5 twice a week with a meal is $1,040 per year.
3. Cut the cord (finally)! Why are you still paying for cable? If this costs an average of $85 per month, it's costing you $1,020 per year.
4. Rotate your monthly subscriptions. If you have at least two streaming services, consider cutting one out for a while and watching items in

the remaining service only. This could save you $12 per month or $144 per year.

5. Go completely without cable or streaming services. My wife and I did this for several years. We utilized our local library to pick up movies and watched some stuff for free on YouTube. Saved an additional $144 per year.

6. Switch from a boutique gym to a traditional gym or rec center. Unless you absolutely need someone telling you what to do, this can save you $50 or more per month. My wife and I attended a boutique gym for about a year at the cost of $180 per month. We got very comfortable with movements and exercises and motivating ourselves. So we cancelled our membership and went to the upgraded subscription at a budget gym, which cost us $40 per month. This saved us $140 per month or $1,680 per year.

7. Cancel gaming subscriptions. These cost about $50 per year. Not huge, but not cheap either. Instead, make your kid go outside, play a board game, or just play the story mode of the game.

8. Avoid in-game purchases. Video games really like to reserve the cool stuff for people that pay extra. Don't fall for this trap. In "Battlefront 2," it was estimated that fully upgrading through purchases alone would cost $2,100.[114] Even if you are spending just $10 a month on this across all games, you could save $120 per year.

9. Avoid app purchases. It was estimated that the average iPhone user will spend $88 in 2020 on app purchases. Since my family got smartphones, we have spent a combined total of $1.97 on app purchases over about six years.

10. Switch to a less expensive wireless phone. We switched to Cricket years ago from Verizon. The coverage is not as good, but it is still better than not having a cell phone like when I was a kid (ok, boomer). We have two lines (my daughter and I, because my wife has a phone through work). An unlimited plan for two lines costs $80 per month (but we are on a slightly limited plan for $70). Compare this to Verizon's unlimited two-line plan for $140 per month. This saves $60 per month or $750 per year.[115]

11. Choose a less expensive vehicle. Experts think you shouldn't have total vehicle expenses exceed 15 percent when buying a car. This

---

[114] https://www.polygon.com/2017/11/15/16656478/star-wars-battlefront-2-content-unlock-time-cost.

[115] https://www.nerdwallet.com/blog/utilities/att-family-cell-phone-plans/.

includes your loan payment, gas, insurance, and maintenance. If you can get this number down even further, great! Instead of a $500/month car payment, you can choose a less expensive vehicle and easily have a good vehicle for $300/month. Don't stretch out your loan term to get lower payments though. Ideally, your loan term should be three years, as most people trade in their vehicle every three-five years. At most, you shouldn't exceed five years. If you are being offered financing for seven–ten years you really can't afford the car, and by the time you want or need to trade it in you will likely owe more than it's worth. A lower car payment of $200/month could save you $2,400 per year.

12. Delay buying another vehicle. Going back to the three–five year average trade-in period, can you push this to six or more years? We just bought my wife a newer vehicle. She drove her last one for twelve years. Save that $300/month on a car payment for a couple of years or use it to pay off other debt. We saved the same amount as we were making on a car payment and used it as part of the down payment on the next vehicle. This saves $3,600 per year.

13. Reduce the number of vehicles you have. My wife and I shared one vehicle for nearly ten years. One of us always lived close enough to work to bike or walk. During those ten years, we did attempt to get a second vehicle at various points, but we were so used to the lifestyle that we couldn't keep two vehicles running. The battery was always dead on one from sitting for too long. This is another way to eliminate a $300/month car payment. This is another $3,600 per year.

14. Staycation instead of vacation. I don't mean stay at home, just modify your plans a bit. One of the best vacation we ever took was a four-day trip to the mountains about two hours from our home. We did all the touristy things we had heard about but never gotten around to doing (one of which I had wanted to see for twenty-five years). The hotel and food were all comparable to anywhere else we would have gone, but we saved the cost of flights for the three of us, which would have been around $1,500 (based on where we had wanted to go). If you do this just every other year, you can save an average of $750.

15. Haircuts can be cut. I had a male friend who insisted on getting a haircut once a month for about $25 plus tip. Before I got married, I was on the six-week schedule (about eight cuts per year) and paying less than $15 plus tip. I then moved to an eight-week schedule (about six cuts per year), which saved me $30 per year. We then got even

more frugal, and my wife started cutting my hair (I do a very basic buzz cut). Since then I've paid for only four haircuts just because she was too busy. This saved me another $90 (on top of the $30 already saved) for a total savings of $120 per year. Compare this to my friend who spends upwards of $300 per year on haircuts. I have to say that I have also learned some basic cutting skills myself to trim my wife's hair, so she gets about only one haircut a year now.

16. Do you continuously run balances on you credit cards? It happens. If you use the cards continuously (rather than switch to cash to pay for things) and don't pay the balance off every month, try calling up your credit card company and asking for a better rate. Some credit card companies are willing to adjust your rate down for a period. When I was buying rentals and financing the repairs on credit cards, I would call up the credit card company and get a better rate for twelve–eighteen months. Then I had balances when the rate expired. I would call up again, and they'd give me a great rate on *new purchases only*. Fine, I used the card for all expenses every month (about $1,500) and always paid about $2,000 on the card. The $2,000 went towards paying off *old* purchases, and the $1,500 were considered new. I estimate that this tactic helped me pay off my cards faster (because more money was being applied to principal each month) and saved about $300–$400 per year in interest.

17. Have balances that you can't get rid of on your credit cards? If you are devoted to just paying your credit cards off, it may actually make more sense to open up *another* credit card and transfer the balance. A lot of credit cards will charge you a fee of about $100–$150 for a balance transfer but then give you twelve–eighteen months zero interest on that amount. If maintained for the whole year, $5,000 on a 19 percent interest rate credit card costs $950 per year. You could save the difference of $850 per year by doing this. Don't have it paid off in a year? See whether your old credit card will offer a similar balance transfer option when time runs out.

18. Don't run the AC. Air conditioning is probably the single biggest user of electricity in a house. As a result, my wife and I use air conditioning only when we are in a hotel. We make do by closing the windows, blinds, and curtains when the sun comes up. This keeps a large chunk of the energy and heat out. At night, we open everything back up. If we need a little something extra, we use fans. This does make for some hot nights here and there and may not be suitable for all climates. Here in Colorado, it is bearable. We estimate that this

saved us about $100–$200 per month for the four hottest months of the year, for a savings of $400–$800 per year.

19. Don't get a pet until you can truly afford it. A dog can cost $100-$200 per month when you add in food, medical expenses, toys, and more. If you are renting you may also be looking at another $100 a month in pet rent as well as coughing a pet deposit of several hundred dollars.

20. Eliminate the private mortgage insurance (PMI). As discussed in chapter 14, this can help you get into a home with less of a down payment. Once you are in the home, you should do your best to eliminate this expense. There are several ways for you to do this. First is to pay down the mortgage enough that it naturally falls off. Often, this is when the amount of the mortgage gets paid down to below 80 percent of the original purchase price of the home. If home prices are steadily climbing and after a few years you think you owe less than only 80 percent of what your home is worth, you can request your mortgage company to evaluate the continued need for PMI on your house. If they feel secure, they can cancel the PMI. Another way to eliminate PMI is to refinance your home with a different lender that feels they don't need it. Beware that refinancing can cost money, and they typically roll in the costs of fees when refinancing. This could set you back a few thousand dollars. Also, be aware of what the new interest rate is. If the rate is higher, it may not make any sense to refinance to eliminate PMI only to have your payment stay the same or increase because the interest has increased. Also beware of repeatedly refinancing into new thirty-year mortgages. Your payment may decrease each time you do it, but you are committing to an additional thirty years each time. PMI ranges from 0.5 percent to 1.00 percent of the loan amount. If your loan is for $300,000, PMI would cost you $1,500 to $3,000 per year or $125 to $250 per month.

21. Switch to inexpensive clothing and buy less of it. I get almost all of my clothing at Ross. The discount retailer sells new clothes at a fraction of what those same clothes cost new. I've gotten good Nike shoes that I drooled over when they first came out for $150 but paid only $45 for them. For jeans, I pay around $20 compared to $50 or more for similar ones at other stores. The average person spends around $161 per month on clothes[116] or about $1,932 per year. I typically buy four pairs of shoes per year and about ten complete

---

[116] https://financialbestlife.com/how-much-should-i-spend-on-clothing/.

outfits plus underwear and socks and spend less than $800 per year, a savings of over $1,100 per year. Take it a step further, and you can buy gently used clothing from thrift stores and save a few hundred dollars more.

Why I Want My Daughter to Know This

These are some of the tricks I have used to save money over the years, but they aren't the only ones. I am constantly looking for ways to cut back costs without sacrificing the quality of my life.

I want my daughter to think about the money she is spending before she spends it. Splurging happens, I am not perfect and have had my share of splurging, but I try my best to be mindful of my spending and be creative with ways to save on the everyday things without sacrificing my ultimate goals.

I hope that my daughter looks around her as she goes through life and makes a conscious decision about what she wants and is willing to spend money on and what is just an expense.

CONCLUSION

I like games a lot. Both board games and video games. I like that there are clearly defined rules to play by. I like that score is kept and you can determine whether you've won. If you know the rules better than others, you have better odds of winning. You know what you can and can't do, and sometimes the rules allow for some flexibility, and that's when your creativity can shine.

For me, money and business are a game. Money is the points system. You can measure your net worth to determine your progress and whether you are winning or losing.

I spent the first part of my career learning how money works. I got a degree in business. I worked for a pay day lender. I worked for a tax preparation company. Then I worked for a bank as a teller, in the finance department, and eventually as a personal and commercial lender. After college I became an avid student, consuming books, podcasts, and courses at a rate that far exceeded what I had done in college. While I did all this, I dabbled in real estate investing.

I was learning the rules of the game as I played the game. Some rules were more painful to learn than others, and I lost money as a result. But I kept playing, learning, and refining my skills. The more I played the game the easier it got. Every new thing I learned about money helped me accumulate more of it, and what I know about money is only a fraction of what there is to know.

I freely admit that I don't know enough about the stock or bond markets. While I invested in cryptocurrencies[117] for a time and understand in theory

---

[117] Cryptocurrencies are a form of money. Most currencies are issued by governments (like the U.S. dollar). Cryptocurrencies were created to be universal money free from the politics that governments are involved in. Cryptocurrencies are limited, whereas governments can always print more of their money, and they are created using a complex computer program called blockchain.

the technology, I know that I could learn so much more. Even in real estate, where I have a lot of experience, there are tools that I have yet to use and investments that I haven't touched.

There are so many possibilities. If you are just getting started, it can be overwhelming, which is why I wrote this book. Having a passing familiarity with the rules of money will help you get into the game and start playing. Don't expect to win the game in a move or two. But if you consistently play, you can end up a winner.

Use this book as a starting point, but I hope you outgrow it. I hope your money grows beyond your ability to manage it on your own and you need a team of advisors and professionals to help you—accountants, lawyers, financial planners, and more.

I wish you success in life.

Go to www.Joshua.Fulenwider.com to get my Quick Start Guide for Setting up Your Child to be Financially Successful.

ABOUT THE AUTHOR

Joshua Fulenwider is a serial entrepreneur devoted to his wife and daughter. At the age of 24, he began investing in real estate, right after graduating from college with a degree in Business Management. He was just in time for the world to fall off a cliff in 2008. Investing in real estate led him to eventually becoming a commercial loan officer and to helping businesses of all sizes. In his spare time, he and his wife love traveling, volunteering, and getting muddy in obstacle course races.